JULIUS DILWEN

WEIGHT LIFTING

The Comprehensive Guide to Weight Training, Learn How to Bulk Up and Increase Your Health Through Weight Lifting

Descrierea CIP a Bibliotecii Naționale a României
JULIUS DILWEN
    WEIGHT LIFTING. The Comprehensive Guide to Weight Training, Learn How to Bulk Up and Increase Your Health Through Weight Lifting / Julius Dilwen – Bucharest: Editura My Ebook, 2021
    ISBN

JULIUS DILWEN

WEIGHT LIFTING

The Comprehensive Guide to Weight Training, Learn How to Bulk Up and Increase Your Health Through Weight Lifting

My Ebook Publishing House
Bucharest, 2021

TABLE OF CONTENTS

Why Should I Lift Weights?

Whether you call it weightlifting, pumping iron, or bodybuilding - lifting weights both light and heavy has long been a great way to get in shape and stay in shape. Weightlifting or weight training has many health benefits for both men and women. There are weightlifting and weight-training routines appropriate for men, woman, even children of any age, any size, and any body type. If you want to build muscle mass, increase stamina, improve cardiac function, even stave off the symptoms of osteoporosis - you can accomplish all of that and so much more by adding a good weight training routine to your regular workout.

To get the most health benefit out of lifting weights, you need to combine your weight training with other exercise. If you are not already doing some kind of aerobic or cardio workout everyday, you must do this in addition to weight lifting. It is not healthy to just begin to lift weights without a proper warm up. Of course before starting any workout routine, check with your doctor. Prior to starting you weight lifting workout you need to "get the blood moving" and your muscles primed for some heavy lifting. Just before hitting the weights do a good ten minutes on a bicycle, take a short jog, or jump rope. Do a few legs and arm stretches as well. The key to successful weight training involves what are called repetitions. In lifting it is not so important how much you lift, but how many times you can lift the weight. A proper weight lifting routine will be designed to work out all of the major muscle groups of the body, which include: The Shoulders, Neck and Back, Biceps, Triceps, Quadriceps Chest, Abs, Hamstrings, Calves, and of course the Gluteus.

The next question on your mind is likely to be "should I use free weights or machines?" and "how much weight should I work out with?" You can use free weights or machines or maybe a little of both. If you are working out in a gym, of course they will have both and will likely be able to recommend a "circuit" of weight lifting exercises for you. If you intend to lift weights in the home, it all depends on your budget and physical space to determine of you want to buy a "Home Gym" type resistance trainer such as Bowflex - or a good set of free weights and barbells - or both. Weight machines are great for beginners because they have been designed to work a specific muscle or muscle group, and will insure that you are seated or standing in the right position to target that group when you lift. Free weights are the traditional barbells and dumbbells that have been around for centuries, and they work great. In fact some would argue that once you learn how to use them properly you get a better workout than machines because it is only the force of your muscles and your ability to balance the weight that keeps the weight and your muscles moving properly. There is no aid from the machine, so you are effectively using more muscle with free weights.

Lifting weights improves your strength and stamina. Lifting weights builds muscle and confidence, improves cardiovascular health and can actually help prevent other sports injuries. And lifting weights can help you lose extra pounds and keep them off - so what are you "weighting" for come on get pumping!

How does Weightlifting Increase Muscle Size?

We all know that lifting weights leads to bigger muscles, harder muscles, and more definition. But just how does weight lifting do that? What is the physiology of weight lifting?

Basically weight lifting is a method of strength training. Lifting weights uses the force of gravity to oppose muscle contraction. Overcoming that opposition increases strength and builds muscle. The concept was simply and elegantly summed up by Hippocrates centuries ago – "That which is used develops, and that which is unused wastes away". He was correct – and his contemporaries while not sure of the anatomical science behind it, also understood the basic weight lifting and strength-training concept of progressive resistance. Its been said that ancient Greek wrestlers when training for the early Olympic Games carried a new born calf on their back everyday until it was grown. While that may not go over very well at your gym, the concept is sound. Weight lifting builds strength and muscle mass through progressive resistance. The reasons our muscles grow and become stronger when we workout with weights is due to the bodies response to injury. Muscle growth from weight lifting is basically a healing process. When we lift weights, we do (when done correctly) a small amount of microtrauma to our muscle tissue. The body's response to the trauma is to rebuild the weakened or torn muscle fibers, and in doing so build them even bigger and stronger then they were prior to the microtrauma so as to prevent repeat of the injury. So that is how progressive resistance works in weight lifting and weight training. We add more weight do more reps, and teardown more muscle fiber - the body keeps responding by healing the muscle eventually pushing the muscle to its ultimate limit, which is genetically determined.

Professional power lifters, other athletes, and experienced weightlifters will use this concept when training or working with weights by adding weight to the point they cannot lift – and then backing off just a bit and then push the maximum weight possible. This is called progressive overload and it forces the muscles to grow stronger and larger to lift the heavier weight. However working out by lifting weights at the ultimate limit of your strength is not recommended for novice weight lifters. Professionals say beginners can achieve the same results a lot

11

safer, by progressively adding repetitions to the workout, and not lifting heavier weights. This will still fatigue muscles, wear down fibers, and result in the progressive microtrauma required to build muscle, strength and stamina.

So what does all this mean? In order for weight lifting to result in building muscle and increasing strength, you must allow the body some down time to "heal". Because it is this "healing" that is really the process of building renewed and strengthened muscle tissue. What that means is that you should not lift everyday – especially in the beginning of your weight lifting regimen. Muscle growth can take anywhere from 2 to 4 days. So beginners generally will workout out every other day. The more experienced you are the longer the recovery period actually can be. Professional or very experienced weight lifters require more strength to push the limit, and cause more damage when they do, and therefore require longer time to build and repair muscles to greater strength. The pros will use a weight lifting routine that works any given specific muscle group only every 4 days.

Basic Weightlifting Equipment

When it comes to exercise equipment, with the possible exception of the jump rope you really cant get much more basic then the gear you need for weight lifting. The first body builders probably just used very big rocks! But seriously, one of the nice thing about weight lifting is not only is it a great way to get in shape, and build strength and self confidence – it does not really require any real fancy or expensive equipment.

Now you can join a gym and have access to all the weight lifting gear you can imagine, both free weights and machines. But you can also accomplish many of the benefits of weight lifting with a basic set of barbells, dumbbells, and a good home work out regimen. Dumbbells usually are the familiar one-piece bone-shaped hand weights. Barbells are usually used for the more advanced workouts and longer muscle groups. This is the long bar with adjustable weight by adding or subtracting weighted plates. Although you can purchase a dumbbell-sized bar, and effectively use plates to make a dumbbell, generally speaking Dumbbells are fixed weights.

For basic weight lifting most pros recommend a 5-50lb Hex Dumbbell set. The hex refers to the shape of the weights – they are hexagonal rather then round, so they will not roll when you put them down. You walls and your toes will thank you. 5–50lbHex sets can be purchased for under 500.00 complete with racks. As far as a Barbell set goes it depends on how much weight you want to have available to you in terms of the plates. And the nice thing about barbells is of course you can always purchase additional weight plates as you lift and increase you abilities. But a decent starter set of Barbells and plates is definitely under 200.00. Garage sales are a great place to find barbells and plates – unfortunately people do not always stick with their commitment to lift weights. A curling bar is also a good idea. Basically a curved barbell (you can use the same plates as on your straight bar) that makes the action of doing curls easier. You also may want to pick up a weight bench. This too can often be found used. A weight bench is essential for doing many weight lifting exercises for the back and chest – and it also can be used for ab crunches, and triceps dips with your dumbbells.

Other accessories you may want to consider are a good pair of weight lifting gloves to protect your hands while lifting. Unless you have a back problem you already are aware of weight belts for additional support are usually not necessary for basic weight lifting workouts. In fact some trainers so they do more harm then good because they allow a lifter to lift more then they really are physically capable of, and cause certain muscles in the forearms and lower back to receive less of a work out and less of a benefit from your weight lift routine. Don't forget that the basic physics of weight lifting is to apply force against muscle contraction to overcome the force of gravity – that same feat can be accomplished by lifting your body weight – and if you are really on a tight budget or pressed for space a simple chin-up bar can be installed in any doorway to get in some lifting and strength training.

Weightlifting and Weight Loss

Can I lose weight by lifting weights? It is a good question. And the answer is if that is the intention of your weight lifting regimen - yes. Now of course in the classic story of the "98 pound weakling" who got sand kicked in his face on the beach and then went on to become Charles Atlas – weight lifting lead to increased muscle mass and weight *gain* - and of course even today many people lift weights to "bulk up". But a properly designed weight lifting workout can be used to burn fat, increase metabolism and *lose* weight.

Doctors and fitness experts agree the key to effective weight loss is to raise what is called Resting Metabolism. Resting Metabolism Rate (RMR) is the rate at which your body consumes fuel when at rest. That fuel is better known as calories. Do you know where the bulk of calories are burned or used in the body – in lean muscle mass. Muscle is active tissue, muscles even at rest burn calories – fat does not. The more lean muscle mass you have the more calories you burn. What is the best way to build lean muscle mass – lifting weights of course! This is why diet alone never leads to permanent weight loss; diet without exercise does nothing to increase RMR. And even the exercises usually associated with sliming down, like aerobics and other cardio workouts, also do little to raise RMR – that is why fitness gurus all suggest adding weight lifting to any exercise program designed for effective and permanent weight loss. This is true for men as well as women. Many women fear weight lifting because they are afraid they will get "too bulky" or "too manly". This is simply not so, Mother Nature has seen to that. Most women just do not have enough testosterone (which speeds and enhances muscle growth, actually making it easier for men to raise their RMR, sorry gals) – to develop a "manly physique". Remember we are not talking about a heavy 2 hour a day pumping iron session. As part of a regimen to raise RMR, moderate weight lifting 2 – 3 times a week is all it should take.

Start out with a weight that is comfortable for you and that you can lift in any given exercise 8-12 times or repetitions. If the muscles do not become noticeably fatigued by the 12th time, the weight is too light, gradually increase until the first signs of fatigue come in at around that 12th rep. To build the most lean mass, gradually increase the weight by about 10% each time you can do the 12 reps. Remember weight lifting is designed to raise RMR and build lean muscle mass as and adjunct to cardio, not as a replacement. They work arm and arm, cardio to burn fat – weight lifting to build muscle mass and increase RMR.

The bottomline is dieting slows metabolism – weight lifting increases it. Dieting plus weight lifting leads to a slimmer healthier you.

Weightlifting Techniques – The Proper Squat

To achieve the proper benefit for any given weight lift exercise you must know the proper techniques and do it right. Incorrect lifting technique can work the wrong muscle groups, or worse result in strain or other injuries. The idea of "no pain – no gain" refers to the burn or the tingle you get when you have worked a muscle to the point that will result in its coming back stronger. Weight lifting is not supposed to hurt, and if it does you are either using inappropriate amount of weight or improper technique.

One of the most common weight lifting repetition exercises is the Squat. The Squat, which can be done with Free Weights or Machines, is one of the best weight lifting exercises there is to build lower body and leg strength. The squat is a weight lifting exercise primarily targeting the quadriceps (thigh muscles) and the glutes. (Rear end). But when done correctly it also works out the hamstrings, the calves, and the lower back. Weight lifters have called the Squat "The King of All Exercises" because it works so many muscles at one time and so quickly builds muscle mass. Ironman Tri-Athlete, Ray Fautex says that if you only had 15 minutes a day to do one exercise make it squats.

The squat is done by bending at the knees and hips and lowering the torso between the legs, and then returning to a standing position. The torso should remain as upright as possible during the bend. In doing squats, keep your back straight. Your feet should be about shoulder length apart. Keep your toes pointed forward. Try it a few times with no weight. If it feels difficult you are probably doing it right. It is absolutely critical to keep the back straight during squats or serious injury to the lower back can occur. If you already have a weakened lower back do to injury a weight belt could be worn during squats to help support the lower back. Feet should remain flat on the floor. To maintain proper balance during the upward motion of the squat, force should be exerted from the heel of the foot and not the toes. If squatting with a particularly heavy weight you should use a squat cage, or have a spotter to help you return the barbell to a safe resting position after the squats.

The most common squat is the back squat – were the barbell is held behind the head, across the upper back. But there are dozens of variants. Such as the Hack Squat where the weight is held behind the legs. The Overhead Squat, which is my particular favorite – squatting while holding the barbell at full extension over your head. There are several Squats where you hold the barbell in front of you like the aptly named Front Squat, where it is gripped with your arms folded across your chest, or the Zercher Squat, where it is held in the crook of the arms.

Squatting is a great weight lifting exercise but by its very nature a very rigorous one. It is recommended that a squat be learned from an experienced weight lifter or professional trainer to avoid potential serious injury.

Weightlifting Techniques – The Proper Deadlift

In weight lifting it is important to know the proper techniques to achieve the desired benefit of a given weight lift exercise. Lifting incorrectly not only can work the wrong muscles but also may cause muscle strain or other injuries. Despite the popular motivational expression "no pain – no gain". Weight lifting when done correctly should not hurt, if you are experiencing physical pain during or after a weight lifting workout, chances are you are using the wrong amount of weight or incorrect technique.

The Deadlift is a popular weight lifting exercise in competition and for professional and personal training. It is the classic weightlifting technique where one grasps a barbell that is on the floor from a squatting position and stands up bringing the barbell to just past the knees. It is the ultimate "test of strength" and is the key movement in competitive powerlifting. While you start from a "squatted" position A Deadlift is unlike a Squat or most other weight lift techniques for that matter, because as its name implies you are lifting a "dead weight". In other words a weight that is not already in motion or other wise already off the ground. It is for this reason that it really puts the muscles to the test, and can also be quite risky if done wrong. The Deadlift works just about every muscle group of the lower body including the abs, the lower back and the back. Other muscle groups involved include the hips, thighs, hamstrings, calves and glutes. To some degree the Deadlift also works the trapeziums (upper back and holders) and the forearms.

To Deadlift, grab the bar with a comfortable grip; legs should be shoulder length apart. Lower body into a squatting position with hips parallel to the floor, back straight, eyes looking forward. Tighten your stomach muscles, and raise yourself and the bar "pushing" with your leg muscles and extending your hips, you are not lifting the weight with your arms or your back. The bar should come to a position above your knees and in front of the hips. Do not round you shoulders. Return the bar slowly to the ground and repeat. The biggest mistake people make in a Deadlift that can cause serious injury is trying to lift with the arms, back, or other muscles of the upper body. While some of these groups will be worked in a Deadlift, the Deadlift is not an upper body weightlifting exercise. To avoid this it is helpful for the lifter to envision trying to push your legs and hips through the floor rather then pulling up on the bar with your arms and back.

The serious risk to improper lifting in a dead lift is back injury. It is imperative to keep the back straight during a dead lift. If you do not this can put stress on the disks and lead to all manner of back problems. A lifting belt could stabilize the lower back and is a good idea if you already have a back condition, however some pros say that lifting belts prevent you from strengthening the very areas that are in need of help in people with back pain.

There are a few variations in weight lifting of the Deadlift, such as the Romanian Deadlift, which is not really a Deadlift at all since in this variation after initial lift, you do not return the bar to the floor. It is designed to work more of the thighs and hamstrings.

The world record for the Deadlift is held by weight lifter Andrew Bolton of Great Britain who pulled 1003 pounds, the first ever Deadlift over 1000 pounds.

Weightlifting and General Fitness

Weightlifting is probably the single most effective exercise you can do to improve health and general fitness. Weightlifting raises your metabolism. Weightlifting builds strength and self-confidence. Weightlifting can improve your game no matter what sport you are active in. Weightlifting improves cardio function and heart health. Weightlifting can even strengthen bones and lessen or prevent the symptoms associated with osteoporosis.

Big or small, short or tall, anyone can benefit and benefit greatly from weightlifting. As we age our metabolism slows down and we lose lean muscle mass and bone density. Loss of lean muscle mass leads to even slower metabolism, and this becomes a vicious cycle leading to on overweight and sedentary lifestyle which brings with it a whole host of other health problems. Now I am not saying that lifting weights and weight training can reverse the ageing process, but it can break this cycle, and make you feel fit and keep you fit at any age. Just ask Jack LaLanne, still going "strong" at 92.

One of the hardest parts of any exercise program is motivation to keep going. It is easier to stay motivated with weightlifting and weight training then most other exercise. Because you can see and feel the result in just a short time. Weight lift for only a few weeks and you will start to see an immediate increase in your strength and stamina by 20 to 40%. And this will not only be in the gym, suddenly all those grocery bags you carry home from the store or your kids are going to feel much lighter. Increased strength and power will improve any sport you are into. Stronger leg muscles will allow you to run faster. Stronger upper body and can hit a ball harder or throw further. Weightlifting and strength training improve stamina overall, and stronger muscles and bones can take more of a pounding so lifting weights can help prevent other sports related injuries.

Of course weight training will help you look better. And many people start lifting only to improve their physique and physical apperance. They do not even realize all of the other benefits one gets from sculpting a toned and defined body by weightlifting. While some fitness experts argue that Aerobic exercise is better to improve cardio vascular health then weight training, studies have proven that cardiac output increases during weightlifting. And of course it is a physiological fact that the heart and lungs support all muscle function, so when muscles are taxed during weightlifting their support system is also getting a workout. That is why today most fitness experts suggest that you engage in an exercise program that includes at least some weight lifting combined with cardio, even a few days a week, for total overall good health and fitness.

Weightlifting and Body Mass Index

One of the ways that medical professionals determine if you are overweight is by a rating called body mass index. BMI is an approximate measure of body fat based on weight and height proportion. BMI was designed to get an approximation or snapshot of body fat – it can over estimate Body fat in those with a lot of lean muscle mass, like weightlifters. BMI is calculated by taking your weight in pounds, multiplying by 703 and dividing that number by your height in inches squared. Compare the results as follows:

BMI Weight Status

Below 18.5 Underweight

18.5 -24.9   Normal

25 - 29.9 Overweight 30 & Abov Obese

Now while it is true that professional weightlifters and especially professional bodybuilders whose regimen and diet is specifically programmed to increase lean muscle for "show" and eliminate as much body fat as possible – can have an inaccurate reading on their BMI. A competitive body builder for example has on average only 4% body fat! But for most of us, if you have not already picked up the sport of weight lifting – and you hit in the 25 or over range on that chart, the truth is there is no better way to lower that BMI and get in shape the weightlifting.

Weightlifting eliminates most of the problems of yo- yo dieting by building lean muscle mass and increasing metabolism. Especially for ageing baby boomers who see those BMI number creeping up and want to do something about it – weight lifting is the way to go.

For weight control it is best to combine weightlifting with cardiovascular workouts, and of course healthy eating. Foods rich in fiber and whole grains and low in fat are the keys to effective weight loss when combined with weight training and exercise. And don't forget to also drink a lot of water. It is important if yo really want to lower your BMI and get in better shape that you combine your weight lifting with cardio work outs. In the first place you should never lift weight without doing some kind of cardio warm up first – just to get the heat and lungs pumping. Also if you are really weightlifting to sculpt a defined and toned body – you need the cardio to burn calories and fat.

In developing a weightlifting routine designed t maximize health, strength, build muscle and reduce your BMI – it is important not to overtrain. That means rotate you muscle groups. And you also need to be aware of primary and secondary muscle groups. What that means is that there are weightlifting exercises that are designed to work a primary muscle group, but since almost all muscles are interconnected they also will train a secondary muscle group. This is the very reason why weightlifting gives you so much "bang for the buck" and a total body work out. For example just about every lift to build chest and shoulders also works the triceps. So if you do triceps on one day, followed by chest the next, and the shoulders the following you will overwork and overtrain the triceps. A good rotation is or split would be: Monday - Chest/Triceps, Tuesday – Break, Wednesday – Back/Biceps, Thursday – Break, Friday – Legs/Shoulders, Saturday & Sunday Break.

Weightlifting and Strength Training

In many articles and in common usage you will hear or see weightlifting and strength training used as if they are the same thing. They technically are not. Weightlifting is a type of strength training, but it is not the only one. The whole idea of strength training is to build muscle mass. Muscle mass is built by forcing muscles to work harder against an opposing force. In weightlifting that force is gravity. You use your muscles to lift either a free weight or a weights on a machine to overcome gravity. But there are other types of strength training too – such as resistance strength training, in which you use the muscle to overcome resistance like that of a resistance band, or resistance machine that uses a series of pulleys. Or Isometric strength training that pits one muscle against another. Still most fitness professionals agree one of the best methods of building muscle is to strength train through weightlifting. And for the purposes of most discussions about how we build muscle and the many benefits thereof, strength training and weight lifting can be considered interchangeable. In fact prior to modern times where much more has been learned about physiology and exercise, and other methods of strength training exercises have been developed, strength training and weight training were pretty much interchangeable terminologies.

Regardless of what you call it strength training and/or weightlifting provides significant health benefits. Strength training builds muscle, strengthens bones and ligaments, and adds to overall fitness and well-being. The key to using weightlifting to increase strength is to use the concept of progressive resistance. You need to continue to tax the muscles by increasing the force they need to work against overtime to continue to build up and gain strength. In weightlifting this is accomplished by either adding more weight or increasing repetitions. Weightlifting is also a great way to strength train because weight lifting exercises, either with free weights or machines have been designed to work targeted and specific muscle groups. So if you want to add strength to your legs because you are a soccer player, you can target leg-lifting exercises, and still receive many secondary benefits of weightlifting and general strength training.

Weightlifting is not however the same thing as Bodybuilding. Popularized by the Movie "Pumping Iron" and rise in fame of Arnold Schwarzenegger, bodybuilding uses similar techniques to weight lifting and carries many of the same benefits, but it is sport with different goals. Most bodybuilders train for open competition, so their goal is to maximize muscularity and minimize body fat. Competitive body builders have from 2- 4% total body fat. A weight lifter or weight trainer on the other hand, is primarily concerned with increasing strength and stamina, and is not too concerned with reducing body fat to below normal levels, and will wind up looking and feeling good by doing that.

Weightlifting for Overall Health

Whether your 8 or 80, weightlifting can be used to improve your overall health. While at one time it was thought that children should avoid lifting weight as exercise because it can cause damage to their maturing bones, and that seniors are just too weak and frail to weight lift. Both of these ideas have proven unfounded. Weightlifting when done correctly can help anyone get and keep fit. There has been very little evidence of bone growth plate damage in children who weight train properly, and seniors well into their 80's and 90's have shown to actually reduce some of the bone loss that comes with aging by working out with weights.

Weight lifting has a multitude of benefits that do not start and end with the obvious of increased strength and more lean muscle mass. We know that increased muscle mass increases your metabolism. Increased metabolism helps you lose weight and keep it off. Weight lifting is also a great natural antidepressant. It relives stress like any strong work out by raising the level of endorphins like dopamine and serotonin, which are known to fight feelings of depression and anxiety.

Basic weight lifting techniques and workouts are usually what are called isotonic exercises, because the muscles are used to apply force to push or pull a weighted object. That object could be anything, but most commonly we are talking about barbells or dumbbells, or weight machines. Weight lifting exercises to gain strength and improve health can be isolation exercises or compound exercises. An isolation exercise is one that is designed to workout or build a specific muscle or muscle group, like a leg lift. Compound exercises are those weigh lifts that are designed to work several muscle groups. Inclined leg presses, where you use both legs to press out to move a weight while reclining on a weight bench is a compound exercise because it involves the quads, the hips, hamstrings, glutes and even can strengthen the knee joints. That is one of the greatest health benefits of weight lifting – many single exercises can be used to work groups of muscles, and produce a great total body workout. Compound exercises are the best to develop increased strength for overall health and daily activities. The muscles worked out in most compound weight lifting exercises most closely resemble the pushing, pulling, bending and lifting we do in our everyday activities, and will make these tasks much easier after just a few weeks of weightlifting. Most of the common weight lifting exercises you are familiar with like the Squat, Deadlift, and Bench Press are compound exercises. Another example of an Isolation Exercise would be the Curl for Biceps. Isolation exercises can be helpful if you want to target a specific muscle group and improve performance for a given sport like your golf or tennis swing, or improving your forearms to help carry around your four year old, as my wife recently discovered!

Weightlifting for Heart Health

Conventional wisdom has been that the best exercise to improve heart health and maintain a healthy cardiovascular sytem and thereby reducing the risk of stroke and heart attack were aerobic or so called cardio workouts. Weight lifting has traditionally been considered an anaerobic exercise, and as such was not thought to be the best choice for heart health. However that is no longer the thinking. Many medical professionals and personal trainers recognize the benefits weightlifting has on the heart and lungs, especially when combined with more traditional cardio workouts.

While up until recently cardiologists actually discouraged their patients from weight training and weightlifting, that view is changing. The American Heart Association published recent evidence that shows the benefits to the heart of working out with weights. The reversal of opinion is not only because physiologists now recognize that there is indeed an aerobic component to weightlifting exercises, but because of the overall improvement in condition and body changes that weightlifting and building muscle create. It has been found that increasing muscle mass and strength actually lowers Resting Metabolism, and resting blood pressure.

While the benefits of building muscle to the body's most important muscle, the heart – are becoming readily apparent for any healthy person – for the heart patient weightlifting and resistance training can be very important to preventing future heart attacks or other cardiac episodes. It is all about being in better condition and being stronger. It's not brain surgery but it is basic heart science. If you have a weak heart even simple tasks like walking up stairs lifting groceries, even walking can put a strain on it. If you are stronger from building lean muscle mass these tasks become that much simpler, your heart doesn't have to work so hard. Studies have also shown that when people lifting weight were monitored for cardiac output the heart pumped stronger and faster. Like any muscle this builds stronger walls in the ventricle, the pumping part of the heart. Strong ventricles mean the heart can pump more efficiently, and effectively lowers resting heart rate, which can lower blood pressure, one of the main contributing factors to heart attack and stroke.

And of course gaining a healthy heart is not the only benefit of weightlifting. Most people who have heart problems are also overweight or struggling with some of the other problems of obesity like diabetes. Weightlifting is a great way to lose weight and keep it off by raising your metabolism and making your body burn calories more efficiently. While minute for minute anaerobic exercises like weightlifting will not burn as much as an aerobic exercise like biking or jogging, in other words15 minute on a stationary bike initially burn far more calories then 15 minutes of weightlifting. However its been found that up to two hours *after* a 15 minute weightlifting workout, the body continues to burn calories as the muscles remain in an agitated state. The American Heart Association now recommends a 30 minute aerobic workout 6 times a week, and adding a weightlifting session of at least 15 minutes 3 times a week.

Weight Lifting for Joint Health

With our ageing baby boomer population, joint pain and joint problems such as arthritis are rapidly becoming major health concerns. Knee, hip and other "load bearing" joint surgeries are becoming increasingly more common. But did you know that a regimen of exercise that includes weightlifting and nutritional supplements like Glucosamine has actually helped some people avoid surgery?

First up we must dispel the myth that workingout with weights can cause joint pain. Now I am not saying that no one has ever left a gym with a sore knee, or shoulder, or elbow, quite the contrary people often do. But if that is caused by your weightlifting routine you are probably doing something wrong. Chances are you are not warming up properly prior to weightlifting, lifting with poor technique, or too much weight, or are not allowing enough time for your joints to recuperate after sets. Here we are discussing the joint pain that can and does occur from everyday "wear and tear", Osteoarthritis or other conditions. Proper weight training has been found to actually improve joint health, return functionality and decrease this pain.

A recent study released in the October 2006 issue of Arthritis Care and Research followed two groups of patients with knee arthritis. One group was given a regular series of Range of Motion Exercises the other a regular routine of Strength Training Exercises, that included weightlifting routines to strengthen the quadriceps and other leg muscles. All patients in the weightlifting group reported less pain then in the ROM group, and more importantly X-rays of those in the Strength Training Group verified that the progression of their arthritis had slowed.

Regular exercise of the joints replenishes joint lubricants and builds cartilage. Weightlifting increases the muscles around joints. Stronger muscles from weightlifting exercises offer more support to the joints. From the process of weightlifting you become physically stronger. This means you can participate in more activities, which make your joints healthier. We already know how weight training builds muscle and how that can improve your overall health and help you lose weight. All orthopedic specialists agree a sure way to reduce joint pain and improve joint health is to lose weight, and ease some of the burden on those weight- bearing joints like the hip or knees.

Simple common weight training exercises have been found to be the best to reduce joint pain of the hips and lower extremities, such as Squats and Leg Extensions. If you are not already weightlifting just as a matter of course to improve health, and are experiencing knee or hip pain, now is a great time to start. Many Americans have totally eliminated their need for ant-inflammatory drugs and other medications to manage their joint pain through weightlifting and strength training. And once you have eliminated your joint pain and start to realize all the other benefits from working out with weights, you can be well on your way on the road to better health and better fitness all around.

Weight Lifting and Back Injuries

Weightlifting is a great way to get in shape and stay in shape. However like many physical activities it is not without its set of risks. Probably the most common injury from weightlifting is back injury. But while back injuries are a potential risk from weightlifting, if they do occur most often they are from poor technique or other errors made by the lifter that can be easily avoided.

There are several possible back injuries that can occur during weightlifting, the most common are stress fractures that occur when flexing the muscles, tendons and ligaments of the back against resistance such as one does during weightlifting. These types of injuries are most commonly caused by improper technique during squats, deadlifts and clean and jerks. Older people who may already be suffering from degenerative disc disease, or people who my already be recuperating from a back injury are particularly susceptible to weightlifting related back injuries. There are several ways to avoid back injuries while weightlifting:

- Know your limitations, do not lift beyond your weight max based on your body condition

- For many exercises it is easier and for those with an injured or weakened back especially, safer to work out using weight machines over free weights

- If you do choose to use free weights, make sure you work with a spotter

- While the use of weight belts for most lifters generally is agreed to have little value, for those with an injured back they can be useful in preventing further injury. Check with your doctor or personal trainer if they think you should use a back belt.

- Do not attempt to do the weightlifting exercises that most often result in back injury i.e.: squats, deadlifts, clean and jerks, without proper training and or supervision.

We've spoken a lot about preventing back injuries while weightlifting, what about returning to lifting after a back injury, one that may or may not have even been caused by lifting? First off you can and will return, but do not expect to return exactly where you left off. You may be able to ease back into you exact routine; you may have to modify your routine to suit you current condition. Only your trainer or spine care professional will be able to accurately advise you. Most fitness pros agree however that after an injury reestablishing that "mind muscle link" that gets the body back into muscle building mode is critically important, and the hardest aspect to the road back. It is best to start slow and ease your body back into bodybuilding gear when coming back from an injury, just as you would do from taking any significant break in your regular weightlifting routine.

Weight Lifting for Kids

There was a time when it was debatable whether kids should weightlift and strength train. The controversy stemmed from the fact that the epiphyseal plates or so-called growth plates, that allow a child to grow, are not closed completely in children and youths. The open distance in these plates is what allows for growth and the thinking was that weightlifting, and certain other forms of physical activity can close these structures prematurely, and impact a child's growth and development. Recent studies have shown that there is no clinical evidence of weightlifting in children causing growth plate injuries. And in fact most personal trainers and family physicians agree that weightlifting and strength training is beneficial to children.

Obesity, especially obesity in children is rampant in this country. Weightlifting fats fight. We know that. Building lean muscle mass is the best way for children or anybody to get rid of fat. Weight training and weightlifting provides a routine and discipline that many children crave and need. Weightlifting in children builds not only muscle but also self-esteem. It teaches children at an early age respect for their bodies and sets in motion good nutrition and good health habits for a lifetime. Speaking from personal experince, this former proverbial "98 pound weakling" who was the target of many a school yard bullies never had his lunch money stolen again after I began weightlifting and strength training in the 5th grade, at the advice of my grandfather, a former Golden Glove Boxer.

The American Society of Pediatrics recently issued guidelines for strength training and weightlifting in adolescents. The report concluded that weightlifting indeed presents no harm to adolescents (other then the same general risks of injury to any weightlifter) and in fact it does lead to increased strength and muscle growth in adolescents and pre-adolescents. The guidelines went on to say that teens and preteens should not lift to their maximum to avoid potential injury to growth plates, and that they should lift a weight that they could comfortably do 12 –15 repetitions with on a given weightlifting exercise.

Now no one is suggesting that your child especially a young one start training like a power lifter. However, studies have shown that children as young as 8 doing a little strength training about 100 minutes a week, not at the maximum weight, but at that 10-12 rep range, saw a drastic increase in strength. It was reported that children in the study, which monitored 8-12 year olds, also showed improvements in eating habits. And interestingly enough parents in the study also reported a noticeable improvement in the behavior and attitude of their children

Weight Lifting for Woman

For many years it was believed that weightlifting was only an activity to be done by men. And even then only by a special breed of males, who wanted to become superhuman examples of human perfection. Even as over the past few decades it has come to be generally accepted that weightlifting is something that has benefits for men other then the muscle beach crowd, still it has generally been looked upon as a male activity. Women fear weightlifting. They think it will make them look too big, or "like men" They think weightlifting is only for the most athletic of women. Not true. Indeed there is a sport of female bodybuilding – but these women will be the first to tell you that they need to work extremely hard, probably twice or three times as hard, to gain that kind of physique as their male counter parts. Why? A simple biological fact – women do not make enough testosterone to build muscle as big or as quickly as men do.

So don't worry about it ladies you can work out with weights and get phenomenal health benefits like losing weight and looking younger – yes I said "losing weight" and "looking younger" – by weightlifting! Lean muscle burns calories. Lean muscle is sexy. There is absolutely no reason why fitness conscious women, and I think today most are, needs to restrict her workouts to just cardio and aerobics. Women can benefit form lean muscle mass as much as men. Biological fact number two – we lose muscle mass as we age, do nothing to replace it, we lose strength and tone and look and feel older. Most Women also know that they are more susceptible to bone density loss than men, so they take calcium supplements. Weightlifting strengthens and builds not only muscle but bones. Studies in women, have shown that resistance training such as weightlifting cannot only prevent but in some cases can reverse the effects of osteoporosis.

Ladies you want shape – you want a figure – building up the muscles of your shoulders and back will make your waist look smaller. And lets not forget about what weightlifting can do for the old Gluteus Maximus. You really want "Buns of Steel"?

– Pump Iron!

Trainers do not suggest that women give up aerobics altogether. In fact a workout regimen that combines traditional

50

cardio-aerobics and weightlifting is ideal. However one more point to note a recent study following women age 24-34 conducted by the Jon Hopkins University found that women who lifted weights continued to burn calories sometimes up to 2 hours longer after the exercise then women who did a comparable period of aerobics.

Weightlifting for Bulk

When people think of weightlifting and building muscle they usually are thinking of two things, "Bulk" and "definition". People will throw around words like I am interested in "building muscle" or and this is especially true of woman, say I don't want to get bulky I just want "to get toned". Further the think bodybuilding is going for "definition and or tone" and weightlifting for "Muscle or Bulk". Well a lot of these terms get misused, even in professional lifting and body building magazines. The truth is that weightlifting, any kind of weight lifting will do both - grow your muscles and tone you muscles. When they talk about definition, or what most people refer to as "Muscle Tone" they really are talking about the muscles you can see, like the six pack abs or bulging pecks. Well in that case Body builders are the ones that are most concerned with showing off their physique as they weightlift for a visual competition – and they know that the way to get "sculpted" and show those muscles has much less to do with how you weightlift as it is with reducing body fat percentage, no muscles, no matter how "toned" will show under a layer of fat.

But if you want to "get big" or weightlift for quote/unquote bulk here is the safe and effective way to do it. Its all about being able to constantly push your muscles to the point that they will continue to grow to their maximum potential which ultimately is determined by your genes. It involves a couple of basic principles, details will vary as you tailor a program to your specific goals and body type, but so long as you train smart, eat right, and get the right amount rest to renew and rebuild – you will bulk up. Period. It's that simple.

First lets set a baseline. Get a tape measure and measure you biceps, quads, abs, every area you want to "bulk up". Also take a picture of yourself. You know all those classic before and after pictures? Follow a program of sensible weightlifting keeping those three basic principles in mind: lift smart, eat right, rest – and you will be that "after guy" (or gal). Set realistic goals for strength or muscle growth. If you can add from a half a pound to a pound of lean muscle mass every week that is good.

A good routine for bulking up means that you should not work any given muscle group more than once a week. The key is to let the body heal and repair that is how muscle growth occurs. When you start lifting of course you will feel sore for the next day or two. Some suggest that you should go back to work that group soon as the pain is gone, but there has been a lot of fitness and medical pros that have said that healing and repairing of muscle tissue that leads to growth and increased strength doesn't happen until after the pain has subsided.

The right diet for "bulking up" when lifting should have a ratio of 40% Protein, 40% Carbs, 20% Fat. Stick with complex carbs, avoid sugars and processes carbs, stick with whole grains. As far as Fats go you know the drill, avoid the bad fats, hydrogenated oils, and trans fats – and stick with good fats like those found in nuts.

Weightlifting and Definition

"Definition" ironically is one of the most improperly defined words in weightlifting and fitness. It is the most misunderstood and misused term out there. I have even seen professional fitness and weightlifting magazines throw around the terms "Tone" and "Definition" indiscriminately and more often then not incorrectly.

When most people use the term "tone" or "definition" they are using it in opposition to the term "bulk". They think bodybuilders are "bulky" the body of a gymnast "toned" and "defined." Poppycock! Nothing can be further from the truth. In fact it is the body builder whose ultimate goal is true "definition". Definition in its purest sense is being able to see clearly "defined" and separated muscle groups. This is exactly what a bodybuilder strives for and competes with.

Yet people think weightlifting especially heavy weightlifting is not for "definition". You will constantly hear

55

people in gyms saying they are not lifting heavy because they are only looking to "tone up" not "get big". Women especially will not weightlift or only lift with repetition after repetition of light weights because they think this will give them "tone and definition". Definition by its true "definition" is less about what weightlifting routines you do, and what weight you work out with, then what you do about reducing your body fat percentage. Muscle cannot be "defined" or look "toned" – if it is hiding under body fat. This is why bodybuilders go for percentage of total body fat in the 2-4% range. And getting to that kind of "definition" is more a function of diet, then it is of any specific kind of weightlifting.

So what are the best weightlifting routines to "tone"," sculpt" or "define" your muscles? All of them. Weightlifting does one thing and one thing only; by pushing muscles to the point of stress it makes the muscle react to the stress by growing bigger and stronger. And yes bigger and stronger means tighter and firmer, but if you want to see that, or want the person sitting down the bar from you to se that - you must reduce the fat. Any weightlifting routine has a fat burning component, and muscle in and of itself burns fat, but if you want to get rid of the fat and be more "defined" that will come from cardio – bike riding, jogging, swimming etc. its that simple. You want to feel and

56

look your best, want to be strong and look great in spandex? Then weightlift to build lean muscle and eat right and do cardio and aerobics to reduce fat.

Weight Lifting and Genetics – is strength and muscle mass determined by DNA?

Nature or Nurture. It has been a debate that comes into play in just about ever aspect of human behavior or ability. How strong, how smart, how fast we are, or can be -are we a product of our environment or genes? Or both? Weightlifters, body builders and fitness pros, are no strangers to this debate.

Anyone can build muscle and reduce fat by lifting weights. So if the question is will your genes determine if you will get stronger or bigger by weightlifting – the answer is no. It does not matter what your genetic proclivities are you will improve you physique and your health by weightlifting. Ultimately how big, or how strong you will get *is* determined by genetics. This is why you can take any two people, with the possible exception of identical twins, put them side by side in the gym, give them exactly the same routines for the same amount of weeks – and they will undoubtedly build muscle and burn fat at different rates. We all know that person, whether they are weight lifters or not - that just seems to be able to eat whatever they want, and stay lean and muscular, never seem to put on weight. While there are others, probably most of us actually, that "just look at food" and you put on fat. This is truly a genetic factor. There are people known as mesomorphs that just have a genetic predisposition towards high metabolic rates – they burn fat easily and build lean muscle easily – so yes such people could be considered "natural bodybuilders".

So what does all this mean as far as weight training goes? Not much really. If you are getting into weightlifting for good health, increased strength and stamina – it doesn't matter if you are a man, a woman, 8 or eighty. No matter what your genetic make-up is you will benefit from weightlifting and building muscle mass to your maximum potential given your genes and your lifestyle. If on the other hand you dream of being a professional bodybuilder or weightlifter then you must consider more closely the hand your genes may have dealt you. Someone who is 5.1 could be very athletic and could become very good at basketball – but it is very unlikely he will ever be able to play starting Center for the Lakers. It is just as unlikely a person with a smaller genetic frame can become a champion bodybuilder. The nature of bodybuilding competitions and what judges usually look for give a major advantage to bigger taller men and women. And the aforementioned "mesomoprhic" types will have a much easier time in training and getting down to the 2-3% body fat champion bodybuilders want to be at.

Bottom line; don't give much thought as to what lies in your genetic makeup. Train hard; push yourself to your limits everyday. Follow a good regimen of weightlifting at least 3-4 days a week, eat right, get plenty of rest, do cardio as well. Look in the mirror in a year or two – and I'm sure you will be very pleased at who is starring back. Certainly you will probably feel better and look better in your *"jeans"* then most people around you - no matter what's in their *"genes"*.

Competitive Weight Lifting

Weightlifting is a great way to get fit. Weightlifting builds muscle. Muscle makes you stronger, burns fat and raises your metabolism. Pound for Pound weightlifting is probably one of the best kinds of exercise you can do for your body. But weightlifting isn't just a hobby or a way to get in shape. It is a competitive sport. And a very exciting one at that.

In fact weightlifting may be the very oldest of competitive sports. The very earliest tests of strength were basically weightlifting competitions. In many ancient societies, the leader of a tribe or group was determined by who could lift the biggest or heaviest rock. Competitive weightlifting as we know it today can certainly traces its history back to the first Olympic Games in Greece. But modern weightlifting competitions as practiced in the Olympics and World Circuit today really had its origins in the "Strongman" competitions of the 19th century. George Baker Windship is generally regarded as the originator of these competitions. The father of modern weightlifting he went on to invent and patent in 1865 what we now know as the barbell and plates.

Weightlifting in the modern Olympics had kind of a spotty history. When the first modern Olympics were held in 1896 it was unsure as to what if any type of weightlifting event ouht to be a part of it. Ultimately it was just two. A dumbbell lift (1-handed) and a barbell lift. (2-handed) In 1900 weightlifting was removed from the program. Weightlifting made a comeback in 1904 returning by means of two entries in the category. Weightlifting again disappeared from Olympic competitions until 1920. It was in the 1920 games that the weightlifting events began to resemble current weightlifting competitions. 1920 was the first time competitors competed in different classes of weight, and they have of course remained. And the idea of medal standing based on an a combined score of three lifts was established. In 1928 these become the standard three weightlifting events, the jerk, the snatch and the press, - and remained as such up to the year 1976, when elimination of the press occured.

Founded in 1905, today competitive weightlifting is over seen by the International Weight Lifting Federation. (IWF) The IWF sanctions weightlifting competitions worldwide including the Olympic Games. There are currently over 150 member nations in the IWF.

In addition to IWF sanctioned events there are many national and regional amateur and professional weightlifting competitions, as well as several "Strongest Man" competitions that continue to gain in popularity. Proving that today like it was in ancient times people like to see men and women pushed to the ultimate limits of human strength and endurance.

Cross Training and Weightlifting

Weightlifting in and of itself is a great sport. But no matter what sport you are into, or whatever you may be training for, there is not a game on the planet that weightlifting cannot improve. We all know how weightlifting can improve general health and fitness, the body benefits in so many ways be increasing strength and muscle mass. But because of the very nature of weightlifting, and the ability to target specific muscle groups with specific exercises, you can cross train by weightlifting to strengthen arms, legs or any other part of the body to perk up your game.

All pro athletes will weight lift as some part of their training routine. Obviously power hitters and other baseball players improve upper body strength with weight training. Ironman triathletes workout with weights doing squats and deadlifts to enhance lower body and leg strength to help in swimming and biking, and not to mention to improve stamina.

Track and field stars will weight lift and weight train because of the way weightlifting promotes lean muscle mass and low body fat percentage. Winter sports are no exception, speed skaters and skiers alike know the benefits of leg lifts and leg presses. And of course football players and wrestlers will strength train and use weightlifting routines and techniques that are almost indistinguishable from a bodybuilders or powerlifter.

So whether you are a pro, semi-pro or someone just trying to get in shape, however you train or workout you are not getting the max if you are not weightlifting too. Cross training just makes sense on so many levels. Variety is the spice of life and so it is true for working out. You will improve health, strength and stamina by cross training No one exercise even weightlifting can "do it all". While of course I have a certain bias toward weightlifting and feel it is the number one all-purpose way to live a happy and healthy life, even lifters have to "cross train". Just for healthy and safe lifting you know we all recommend doing 15 – 20 minutes of aerobic exercise prior to ever lift session. That right there is "cross training". Also if you really want to get and keep a lean and mean physique, weightlifting alone won't do it. It doesn't matter how tight you make that six pack – no one will see how ripped it is if it hiding under a layer of body fat. Cross training with cardio will help to burn fat.

Now I know a lot of you get really psyched up about lifting, and there is no greater natural high then after you get those endorphins flowing after a good pumping session, but lets face it, weightlifting, like any exercise routine, if you do the same thing over and over again can get a little boring. Cross training gives you the opportunity to not only improve overall health and fitness, but shake things up a bit and break from your routine so it doesn't get tedious.

As with any exercise routine before you plan on adding any kind of cross training activity to your current workout, check with your healthcare professional or personal trainer for its suitability.

Weight Lifting as Physical Therapy

Do your know were many peoples first introduction to weightlifting is? It is not in a gym, it is in a Physical Therapy room. In fact if I walked you in blindfolded to either a modern gym, or modern PT department of most major hospitals or orthopedic centers, I bet you would be hard pressed to tell them apart. Weightlifting is almost always part of the physical therapy to recuperate from an injury or slow the effect of joint disease such as arthritis.

There is a common misconception that people with an injured back, or hip, or knee pain due to arthritis, bursitis or other degenerative joint disease, should not weightlift because it will only make the matter worse. Not true. Weightlifting is not only an accepted practice in physical therapy, but a recent study published in several medical journals proved the benefits of weightlifting and strength training to patients with knee arthritis. For many people with chronic hip and knee pain a regimen of exercise and physical therapy that included weightlifting prevented the need for joint replacement surgery.

Weightlifting, like all strength training is a type of Progressive Resistance Exercise. The physiological definition of Progressive Resistance is a method of increasing a muscles ability to operate against force. In lay terms that means it is the way we get stronger. The main reason that someone is undergoing treatment by a Physical Therapist is that a muscle or joint due to disease involvement, injury, or genetic defect cannot generate enough force to engage in everyday activity. The goals therefore of the Physical Therapist and the Weightlifter are the same, to strengthen muscles. There are several major disciplines of Physical Therapy including musculoskeletal, neuromuscular, and gerontology. That's Muscles and Bones, Nerves and Anti-aging. There were some interesting results in a recent survey published by the National Library of Medicine and The National Institutes of Heath. The survey was designed to determine the effectiveness of progressive resistance exercise as a part of physical therapy. And it was found that across disease conditions and injuries weight training and Progressive Resistance Exercise made a major difference in a patient's ability to generate force with the affected joint or muscle being treated. Furthermore it was determined that these improvements carried over into everyday life.

However one of the other conclusions of that same study was that with many of the injuries, the initial benefits gained by weightlifting as part of physical therapy, dissipated after the therapy was completed. So what does this tell us? Not that we wish pain or injury on anyone, but PT can be a first introduction to the benefits of weightlifting and strength training, and that anyone who has had PT should be encouraged to carry on with progressive resistance exercises like weightlifting throughout their lives. This will not only maintain the improvements gained from the physical therapy, but can get you into a practice that has been proven to have a positive effect on overall health and fitness, and could very well help to prevent a repeat of the very injury that put you in PT in the first place.

Weight Lifting and Stress Management

Stress. We all deal with it day to day. Most mental health and other healthcare professionals agree that one of the best ways to deal with and overcome stress is to raise the endorphin level in the brain and stimulate the "pleasure centers through rigorous exercise. The so-called "natural high". And there is none better that I can think of than the one you get after pumping up from weightlifting. The very term "pumping up" and feeling pumped after weightlifting refers as much to your state of mind, as the state of your muscles.

Lifting weights reduces stress in many esoteric and practical ways. Physiologically there is no doubt that a heavy duty workout with weights raises the levels of dopamine and serotonin – two chemicals in the brain known as neurotransmitters. These are the two that are most related to depression. In fact most antidepressant medications work by increases the level of both of these chemicals in the brain. A good weightlifting session can accomplish the something, without the side effects, and has so many more additional benefits to both your physical and mental health. Stress relief though weightlifting is more then just the high you get after a work out, and a good way to let off steam and release the tensions of a heavy duty day. The additional benefits one gets from being a weightlifter can go along way to reduce and manage stress. Better health, the ability to be more active, improved self-image and confidence all come from weightlifting -and can do a lot to fight stress and depression. I know of many people who began a weightlifting program strictly to "get in shape", and then found how it improved so many other aspects of their lives. One of the great things about weightlifting is unlike with many other types of training you can see results almost immediately. Many people who never lifted before in just a few weeks of weight training see a dramatic improvement in their strength and stamina, and even start to see a difference in the mirror in a short time. This leads to improved self-esteem, which can and has led to all sorts of positive changes in ones life. Now certainly I am not suggesting that weightlifting is some magic genie in a bottle that will immediately improve you life. But, with increased self confidence and self esteem that comes from improved health and self image from a regular weightlift routine, people have gone on to find partners and even find better jobs. In other words you have so much to gain with weightlifting and so little to lose, except some flab! And speaking of meeting people, if you workout in a gym, weightlifting is an inherently social activity, many weightlifting routines require spotters or partners, and lifting is a great way to meet people. Being active socially is also a great way to relive stress.

Now I have primarily been talking about weightlifting and relief of mental stress. But muscles also suffer from physical stress. This is when trainers and healthcare professionals refer to "tension" in muscles. Or when you yourself say your lower back, neck, or shoulders feel "tense". This is a great time for a lighter work out with weights, the simple warm-ups and stresses that must be done before a weightlifting session could start to loosen up this "muscle stress", followed by a workout with lighter weights and it will melt away, and those endorphins will also get going and the rest of your stress will start to fade along with it.

Weight Lifting and Discipline for Teens

If you are the parent of a "troubled teenager" – you may be at your wits end of what you can do to help them. Many child behavior specialists agree that for a teens with certain behavior problems especially those related to attention deficit or defiance disorders, the routine of a regular exercise regimen can do wonders. Weightlifting can be a perfect activity for this. Weightlifting can help focus a teen's attention. It can teach him or her about setting goals and obtaining them. Weightlifting can give a teen focus, an outlet for stress and other aggressive emotions. Weightlifting in a gym environment can teach teens about cooperation and working with others as they spot for other lifters. Building muscle builds self-esteem and confidence two aspects of personality that experts agree are often found lacking in teens with depression or other problems.

Teens who become involved in weightlifting are more likely to participate in other physical activities. And weightlifting will improve their skills in any other sport you can think of. One teen from Summit New Jersey, who says she started lifting at 14 years old, is now 18 and says she is in "incredible" shape. Her lifting gave her the confidence to start taking lessons in her other passion Jazz Dancing, and has enhanced her skill their many fold. She says weightlifting for teenage girls is great - it can keep them in shape, looking and feeling great, and avoid crazy diets and eating disorders.

Experts say developing the discipline associated with a sport like weightlifting can teach teens the importance of keeping their bodies fit and minds mentally alert and can provide a good instructional model for avoiding drug or alcohol abuse. A teen who works with a personal trainer that teaches them to respect their body, is far less likely to abuse it. The importance of having your teen, especially if he or she is seeking the therapeutic effects of weightlifting work with a professional personal trainer cannot be understated. If there is a "dark side" to teens and weightlifting it is that there have been abuse of anabolic steroids by teens who want to grow faster and get bigger. The best way to avoid this to be sure your youth works with a responsible and certified personal trainer.

Of course as your teen becomes a weightlifter he or she will experince all of the physical benefits of weightlifting, and not just an improved outlook on life. Besides the other obvious physical benefits of improved strength and muscle tone, a recent study found that the incidence of diabetes is on the rise in teens. According to a study conducted by The University of California, teens at risk of diabetes could significantly lower that risk through weightlifting and strength training exercises. In people who are overweight especially teens, insulin resistance is a precursor to diabetes. Insulin resistance is when the body does not process insulin properly. The study followed teenage boys who lifted weights twice a week for 16 weeks and concluded that there incidence of insulin resistance was drastically reduced. Of course the study found in the same group of boys that the weightlifting also increased lean muscle mass and decreased body fat percentage.

Weightlifting with Free Weights

Weightlifting is the theory of building muscle by applying force to a weight to overcome the force of gravity. Its the idea of putting stress on a muscle, the way the body reacts to that stress is to overcome it by making the muscle stronger. The weight can be a "free weight" like a barbell or dumbbell or a weight machine.

Free weights for weight lifting have been around probably since the first ancient human picked up a large rock. In fact the earliest "tests f strength" to determine rank in primitive tribal cultures consisted of just that, who ever could lift a certain rock was deemed strong enough and worthy enough to be named "chief'. Free weights have become slight more sophisticated over the years, yet are still the most economical and easiest way to build muscle through progressive resistance training. Some would argue they are the purist form of weight training and therefore the best. They say that using free weights in proper form has its advantages of weightlifting machines because weight is being driven by all muscle; there is not point in the lift where the machine "takes over".

Free weights are cost effective, you can use them almost anywhere, when I used to travel extensively as a reporter and wound up in a hotel that did not have a gym or exercise room, I packed a pair of dumbbells that fold flat and can be filled with water! Free weights allow you to do the widest variety of weightlifting routine and exercise with just a small set of barbells and plates. Just about every major weight training exercise can be done with free weights s and the addition of a weight bench. "Pound for pound" your muscles get a better work out then with most weigh training machines, as does your entire body. When using free weights,, during upper body exercise for example you must use your legs and back muscles to balance and stabilize the body, this working these groups as well.

Technique is critical when working out with free weights, it is beyond the scope of this one article to teach you proper technique on every free weight exercise. It is best to join a gym or work with a personal trainer. However if that is not within your budget there are many sample routines and instruction bodybuilding and weightlifting programs that can be found and downloaded online. There are also several very good instructional weightlifting tapes and DVD's out there. As with any exercise program you should consult with your physician or healthcare professional before starting to work out with free weights. Other things to remember when using free weights is to always exercise both sides of the body. Progressive resistance can be accomplished just as well by increasing the amount of reps on a given routine as by increasing weight. You must give your body time to rest to build muscle and therefore need to rotate the muscle groups you are exercising with your free weights, and take a break entirely from weightlifting at least one or two days a week.

Weight Lifting With Machines

One of the most common question people will ask when it comes to weightlifting is "ShouldI use free weights or machines"? It is a good question, and one open for debate. Both weightlifting with machines and weightlifting with free weights have their pros and cons. And advocates on both sides. There are those that swear the only true work out must be done with free weights, yet for those who are novices or have had certain injuries, machines seem to be the ticket. Actually most fitness professionals recommend a combination of both, but if you are intimidated by the idea of barbells, and like the more modern feel of weight machines, you can and many do, train exclusively on machines.

If you plan to weightlift only on a machine you will likely be doing most of your workouts in a gym. While there are some good home gym universal or nautilus type machines available, they are not inexpensive, and they do require a fair amount of space, certainly more than free weights. The main advantage of working out with a weight machine is that you do not have to be as conscious of technique. So they are excellent for beginners. Working out with free weights requires far more training, it is less likely you will injure yourself with an incorrect body position on a machine, because basically the machine positions your body for you. Machines are very easy to use and require little or no training; the movements are "preprogrammed " on a fixed path based on the mechanics of the machine. Most can hop on a machine and use it correctly the first time by simply reading the instructions with pictured diagrams that are affixed to every machine. Machines are very good for weightlifters that have a limited range of motion for any reason, many of the same exercises that somebody with such problems could not do with free weights they can do on a machine. Many feel that "circuit training" is easier on machines, and because they are easier to use, people use them longer then they do free weights. Now some will argue that minute for minute you get a better workout with free weights, and that may be true, but some people *feel* better about themselves if they can work out longer. And in weightlifting feeling good about what you are doing and accomplishing is part of what its all about. Also as far as time goes, with machines because you don't have to change barbell

80

plates simply shift a clip to change weight, you spend more of your time actually workingout.

If you are rehabilitating from an injury especially of the back or shoulders the added support that machines provide can mean the difference between getting back into weight training or not. Also machines are great for the "loner" at home or in the gym, the person who wants to work out with heavy weights and not worry about a spotter is ideally suited to use a weight machine. You can lift to the max on a weight machine with no fear of dropping the weight on yourself and causing serious injury.

Best Home Gyms for Weight Lifting
and Strength Training

Today more and more people are foregoing a gym membership and choosing to weightlift and strength train in the comfort and privacy of their own homes. While a set of dumbbells is probably the most cost effective way to do so – more and more people with the space and the budget are opting for a home gym machine. Universal type home gyms or circuit trainers are not cheap, however the prices have come down over the years. There are some very good home gyms for weightlifting that are under 1000.00. Most major manufactures offer some kind of financing, so for the cost of a monthly gym membership – if you prefer to train at home, you can have a quality home gym.

Just as the approach to all things weightlifting when choosing a home gym, it is best to identify your goals before you start to shop around. What are your looking to weightlift for? Do you want to bulk up, or are you going more for tone and definition? Are you recuperating form an injury and can no longer work with free weights but want to keep a program as close to your original weightlift routine as possible? The answers to such questions will help narrow your focus to the type of machines your are looking for. There are basically two categories of home gym for weightlifting. One is the multi-exercise workout stations weight stack machines - basically a scaled down home version of what you will find in the gym – and resistance trainers that do not use weights at all – like a Bowflex. While the second is not technically "weightlifting" since no weights are involved, it still uses the same ideas of progressive resistance and strength training; and can achieve in many cases the same kind of results as working out with free weights or weight machines. Budget and space is of course another consideration either one of which can be the ultimate limiting factor on what type of machine you can purchase. For space issues the resistance trainers are probably the way to go – many strength training exercises can be done on a Bowflex, they take up very little space, and there are several versions designed to fit most budgets, and financing is available.

As far as a workstation goes, a very good one for less than 1000.00 that does not require that much space is the Body Solid

EXM-1500S Home Gym. The Body Solid allows for all of the major weightlift routines and workout stations including a low row. Because they place the low row off to the side, rather then in front of the press bench where it is on most machines, the Body Solid takes up a little less room. It has a 160 lb weight stack, is scratch and dent resistant, and includes a Lat Pull down bar, Shortbar, Ankle and Ab Crunch straps. It comes with a lifetime warranty and can be purchased at a good price point. If you are a real heavy power lifter you may want more then the 160-pound stack, but for the beginner and most weightlifters it is it is a great machine.

Weight Lifting on the Road

It's a dilemma many of us workout heads face. How do I stick with my routine when I am traveling? I know several avid weightlifters who plan there business trips around their "off days". But not everyone has that luxury and we all know how hard it is to comeback after any kind of significant break from lifting. But there are a few ways to weightlift on the road so that you do not have to miss a single squat.

First up, as a reporter as you might imagine, I have had to travel quite extensively throughout my career. There are many inexpensive hotel chains that have fitness room as part of their amenities, just about every high-end hotels will. But I have found that most Hampton Inns, Holiday Inns, Courtyards, and Fairfield Inns have Fitness Centers. Just be very careful about what they refer to as a fitness center, I have found several that have multi-station weight machines, along with a dumbbell rack – but many that list "Gym" or "Fitness Center" in their amenities only mean they have a treadmill and an exercise bike. So call ahead and see what they have and if it is in working order. Also many national gym chains offer memberships that will allow you to workout in any of their locations, and of course most major gyms will offer you some kind of "day pass" to workout.

But if you find yourself in the middle of nowhere, and none of those option will work, don't panic there are still some things you can do to keep pumping. First of all planning is everything. While sometimes you can't predict where you will be and what if any gym equipment you will have access to, if you know you are going to be in a place with limited workout time or gear – increase your workout to the max before you leave. While we usually recommend against overtraining, under these set of circumstance it makes sense – this way if you have to take time off – your body will need it!

OK so what can you do if you are on the road, in a hotel with no gym, and no gym nearby? Wake up people; long before barbells the powers that be made Push-ups! And you know what? They still work to build muscle and burn fat. Hotel Rooms also all have chairs –dips between chairs are a good workout. Also for cardio you can pack a jump rope. And don't forget running up and own the stairs. You can simulate a low row by putting your legs beneath a rail or bed and pulling yourself up and towards it. If you can find something solid to hang from (NOT the shower rod) you have a pull-up station. On a long trip and not traveling "light"? – Use your luggage to do arm curls gripped at the handles! Be creative you can do wall sits and lunges against a table for legs and thighs, and of course don't forget sit-ups and crunches.

Bottomline? While it can be tricky to stay in shape and weight train on the road it is certainly not unfeasible. Be creative, use the materials at hand and above all eat right, avoid the all you can eat eggs and bacon breakfast buffets and fast food, and you can keep up with your fitness goals even when traveling.

Best Weight Lifting Videos

Weightlifting and weight training especially with free weights requires training and instruction for proper technique. Weightlifting with improper techniques can cause many problems from simply not stimulating the targeted muscle groups to serious injury. But not all of us can afford a gym membership or a personal trainer. For them a good set of barbells and a quality instructional video is all they need.

There are dozens and dozens of good quality weightlifting videos out there. Again as in any discussion in weightlifting, you must first clearly identify your goals, what is it you are trying to accomplish? What ever it may be from packing on the muscle for competition bodybuilding, to building lean muscle mass for definition and overall health, there is an instructional video made by a well-known fitness professional that can teach you what you need. Just search Amazon or eBay and you will get 100's of results. There are Weightlifting for Seniors videos,

Weightlifting for Woman, Weightlifting for Kids, and even though I do not particularly recommend this practice for the amateur lifter, even videos of both Men and Woman Weightlifting in the nude.

Here are some of the best in no particular order.

- See one of the greats on *Kevin Leverone's Maryland Muscle Machine Body Building Video*. Kevin is a former Mr. Olympia and you can see his marvelous form and technique on this video. Kevin's is known for his workouts with extremely heavy weights, and on this video you will be amazed as he does 1500 pound leg presses and 100 lb dumbbell single arm curls.

- On the Other end of the spectrum is *The Complete Weight Training Series by Joyce Vedral*. Designed for Women Fitness Guru and NY Times best selling author Joyce Vedral takes you through fat burning and cellulite busting workouts with weights. A series of videos that introduces women to weightlifting and keeps them going through a series of progressions that will build muscle, burn fat and improve bone density.

- One of the most definitive and respected body building videos is put out by Iron Man Magazine. It is called *Critical Mass Body Building for the Beginner and Intermediate*, and it details the new sensation that is taking the bodybuilding world by storm, Flexion. It explains in detail the theory behind Flexion, and how to use these techniques to build more muscle, bigger and faster without the use of steroids.

If you are interested in not only videos for instructional purposes but would like to see a great behind the scenes look at the Mr. Olympia competition, current Mr. Olympia, Jay Cutler has a great video out. Its called *One Step Closer*, and it is a 6 hour documentary that starts 4 weeks prior to the 2005 competition and take you through Jay's training, pre-judging and victorious finale.

And if you have looked at a completely ripped body builder and said – "I cant do that" or "I can never look like that" – then you must see *Freak of Training – The Adam Archuleta Story.* Adam was a scrawny kid determined to play for the NFL – a small walk on player in college, against all odds he got into a weightlifting and strength training routine that increased his speed, strength and stamina that made him a First Round Draft Pick!

Best Online Weight Lifting Courses

Training and learning proper techniques is the safest way to weight lift. You can get books that illustrate the basic weightlifting exercises, and offer some really good weightlifting workout programs. There are 100's of weightlifting and strength training videos available. But probably the closest thing you can get to a personal trainer if you cant afford to go that route - is an online. "virtual trainer" There are many very good Online Weightlifting Courses available.

On such site is Online Gym America (www.gymamerica.com) there you get to plug in a few basic stats about yourself and yo will receive a free fitness profiles and recommended workouts, then for a small monthly fee you will be given a customized weightlifting and workout plan designed for you specific body type and fitness goals. Their online Total Fitness Virtual Trainer uses specialized software to create customized individual workouts. With an outstanding level of interactivity programs such as these react to your improvements and modify your program accordingly. The are over 100 detailed and easy to follow animations so you ail be sure you are performing each weightlifting exercise correctly. There is also an online nutritional counselor that will help you design a diet and meal plan that corresponds to your weightlifting routines and bodybuilding goals.

You can sign up for free online weightlifting and strength training course at www.ast-ss.com

There you will find a specific training course that takes a no-nonsense approach to bodybuilding using the latest in the state-of-the-art technologies of supplementation, weightlifting, and biofeedback to build muscle fast and accurately. This online course is a program that progresses over the course of several weeks teaching you the real facts behind weight training and teaches you how to build lean muscle and reduce body fat the way the top professional athletes and bodybuilders do. Beginners and experts have benefited from this online weightlifting program, that offers guaranteed results.

Woman can find what they are looking for in an online virtual weightlifting trainer at www.strongwomen.com . Based on your needs and body type, there you will find weightlifting programs designed to build bones, keep you trim and slow the effects of aging. Also check out the site of Roger Power. Roger Power (yes I believe that is his real name) is a certified Personal Trainer and world class bodybuilder. He offers an online virtual trainer that takes his holistic and natural approach to weightlifting and body building, that he teaches in person into cyberspace at www.femalemuscle.com

Today we can pay our bills online, meet the love of your life online, even make a living by never leaving your home on line, and believe it or not you can keep a lot more then just your fingers in shape by checking out an online weightlifting and fitness program.

Weightlifting Accessories

Weightlifting is more than just a great way to stay in shape; in fact it is more than just exercise it is a sport. There are both pro and amateur competitive weightlifters, not to mention bodybuilders. And like any sport weightlifting has its share of accessories. Here are some of the essentials.

When we are referring to weightlifting accessories we are talking about anything other then the weights themselves. This can be any piece of equipment or gear that makes the lifting experience easier like weightlifting gloves, to things that help you build up like nutritional supplements. Weightlifting gloves are something that should be worn by any lifter, they prevent blistering and other damage to the hands, and insure a better grip on the weight bars for better form and technique and reduced risk of injury from slippage. Your feet deserve similar protection and there are weight lifting boots. They help provide better balance and a more stabile platform for lifting as well as protect the feet from injury. Other types of safety related weightlifting accessories include weight belts and, wrist straps. An ingenious weightlifting accessory in this class is the lifting hook. Lifting hooks have been made to stabilize the wrists and relive stress on hands and wrists while insuring proper bar handling. There are accessories both large and small for specific types of lifting exercises, like weight benches, and head harnesses.

Other accessories include pieces of gear designed to complement or enhance your workouts. Specialized bars fall into this category like curling bars, as do accessories like ankle and wrist weights. A simple yet effective and very popular accessory in this group would be a wrist roller. Basically a dumbbell bar with a cable that you hang a weight plate from and then roll it up. It is probably one of the single most effective ways I know of to strengthen your wrists and forearms, and can be done anywhere.

Then there are other pieces of equipment that are not technically used in actual weightlifting, but are used in complementary exercises that are usually part of a weight-training program. These include, chin up, and pull up bars, push up bars, chest toners, and the ever-popular handgrips and skip ropes. Other weightlifting accessories include those that make your home gym easier to manage and more organized. This would include things like dumbbell racks, plate trees, and other kinds of accessory racks.

Whatever type of weightlifting accessories you are in the market for from a simple set of spring clips for you barbells to a press bench or beyond, there are dozens of discount sites online that sell all sorts of weightlifting accessories at deeply discounted prices.

Fashions for the Weight Lifter and Body Builder

Guy or gal you work hard as a weightlifter or bodybuilder to get ripped. And we know your greatest pleasure is to show off the fruits of your labors, whether that is in competition, in the gym or on the beach. But lets face it – though you may want to, you can't just walk around in a speedo or a thong in the office or down at the super market. But that doesn't mean you cant wear clothes that are comfortable and make you bod look great no matter where you are day or night.

Actually before we get into high fashion for the weightlifter. Lets take a look at the more practical side and talk a little bit about the clothes you need to wear while working out. Now if you're a guy like me and basically work out at home you probably are just in any old sweatshirt with the sleeves ripped off, and a pair of shorts. But in the gym you may want something a little more stylish like a form fitting Y-back Tank Top. Couple that with a pair of baggy workout pants like the

O500 Red Dragons from Otomix, and you'll be stylin' Of course women want to look their best wherever they are and for them weightlifting fashion is designed to make them true "bar belles" with everything form sports bras with matching head and wrist bands, to gym bags with accessorized towels and key chains.

On the practical side both men and woman should consider wearing fitness or specially designed workout shoes during weightlifting. These improve balance and stability while lifting, but are also designed to be lightweight enough to be used for cardio before weightlifting sets. And many of them also look damn good.

Now to the other side. You've worked for it you've got it – flaunt it. There are complete lines of fashion wear made specifically for active physically fit guys and gals. Usually called "club wear" look for a lot of spandex and use of other materials specifically used to fit the athletic body. One company in particularly called Hot Bodz Clothing offers a complete such line for weightlifters and body builders. Their fashions include not only the aforementioned club wear, but also contemporary fashions specifically tailored to better fit the muscular physique. Form fitting club shirts in a variety of colors and patterns, look as good elbowing up to any che che bar as they do just walking along South Beach. There are also denim and leather jackets cut specifically for the weightlifter to make you look your best day or night. There are even dress shirts made of a fabric called stretch poplin that can make you look as good in the boardroom as the weightroom.

So whether working out or hanging out as a weightlifter or bodybuilder there are clothes that have been designed to make you look your best.

Weight Lifting and Nutritional Supplements

You cannot open a weightlifting or muscle magazine without seeing dozens of ads for nutritional supplements. And truth is if you want to bulk up faster and put on weight, supplements can help. But it important not to believe all the hype. While nutritional supplementation can help with building muscle, there are no short cuts, and no substitutes for proper training and weightlifting.

The idea of nutritional supplementation for weightlifting and bodybuilding is a simple one. We know that there is a basic equation to building muscle through weightlifting and resistance training: push your muscles to their limits, followed by appropriate rest to build new muscle, and give your body the proper nutrients it needs to build muscle. Supplementation comes in at that last part of the equation. While many lifters can develop a good routine of "on again/off again" training and can stick to it – always eating the right foods that give the body what it needs to build muscle and build muscle quickly isn't always that easy. Supplements make sure you are giving the body what it needs to recover and build muscle after workingout.

Nutritional supplementation for the bodybuilder or weightlifter fall into a few categories, and once again how you supplement will depend on what your ultimate weightlifting goals are. Nutritional supplements for weightlifters are usually products designed to increase muscle like proteins and creatine. Products designed to increase metabolism like fat burners. Supplements that safely simulate the effects of harmful anabolic steroids, and products that aid in recovery and promote joint health like Glucosamine and MSN.

Protein is one of the most essential building blocks to making new muscle. It is cannot be stored in the body so to build muscle you need to constantly replenish your bodies supply of protein. Unfortunately the foods that are highest in protein are often also the highest in fat, and as a bodybuilder or weightlifter you are always trying to decrease your fat intake. Also you are probably loading on carbs, and again most foods high in carbohydrates are low in protein, so most weightlifters will supplement with a good quality protein powder. Protein powders come in variety of types – such as whey protein or soy protein - and flavors, and can be used not only in drinks but in recipes like those found in the Zone diet. Check with your personal trainer or healthcare professional for the right protein supplement for you.

Protein builds muscles, a chemical known as ATP, Adenosine Triphosphate is the fuel that powers them. One of the other most popular supplements that is taken by weightlifters is Creatine. Creatine is naturally found in meat and fish. Creatine when it gets into the muscles combines with phosphate and creates ATP. The more ATP the stronger the muscle and the more resistant it is to fatigue. ATP gives the muscle bursts of energy that allow you to weightlift longer and stronger.

And finally there are the supplements that are the so-called anabolic alternatives. We all know about the dangers of steroids. To avoid the potential problems of taking steroids but to achieve the same type of effect safely, these products all basically work the same way. They use a combination of herbal and other natural ingredients to naturally enhance or stimulate the body's own production of testosterone. And while these products are generally safe, and do not involve the ingesting of hormones, since the are intended to and can change the levels of hormonal activity in the body they should still be used with precaution by teens and women.

Best Protein Powders for Weightlifters

Protein is an essential nutrient for building muscle, and therefore it is an essential part of any weightlifters routine. But protein is not stored in the body, and since it is used to build muscle, the more your build up, the more protein you use, and the more protein you need. It is difficult if not impossible for serious weightlifters to take in all the protein they need to build all that muscle. Most foods that are high in protein are also very high in fat, and as weightlifters or bodybuilders you always want to limit your fat intake. Also most heavy duty lifters have a diet that is high in carbs to bulk up and provide energy – again foods that are high in carbohydrates, are usually low in protein. So most weightlifters will get their protein form shakes made with protein powders.

Protein powder formulations used by weightlifters usually have one of two sources of the protein, soy and Whey. It seems in recent years more weightlifters prefer the Whey protein powders. There has been some evidence that Soy and Soy products limit the production of Testosterone, which is the last thing you want to do as a weightlifter trying to build muscle. Whey protein also has been shown to improve liver function, boost the immune system and act as a natural anti-bacterial and anti viral. Whey protein has what is called a very high biological value. Biological value is the amount of protein your body replenishes per 100 grams of ingested protein. If you are interested in protein being used to build muscle, you of course want the highest BV possible. Unlike soy protein, which is derived form a vegetable source, soybeans; whey has a high BV because it derived from milk. "Pound for Pound" or actually in this case "gram for gram" the only source of protein with as high a BV as whey is eggs, but whey does not have the fat or cholesterol component of eggs.

Whey protein is also high in essential Amino Acid, which are also important to weightlifters.

Whey protein powders are available from several different manufacturers. Whey protein powders either come unflavored, or can be mixed with any food or juices, or in a verity of flavors to make shakes and drinks. But since it comes form cows milk in a recent survey many people preferred the taste of even unflavored whey protein over other protein powders, probably because it is derived from milk. Really it becomes matter of personal taste when it comes to choosing any single whey protein powder over another. Any whey protein from any manufacturer is ideal as a weightlifting supplement because it is high quality protein with no fat, no lactose, no cholesterol, is all-natural and is low in calories.

Weightlifting with a Personal Trainer

Weightlifting, especially if you are going to be using free weights, is not something that should be approached without getting proper training or instruction first. Most injuries that are reported due to weightlifting, or most reasons why people fail to achieve the goals they are going for, are because of improper weightlifting technique. While you can and many do, learn the basic techniques of the basic weightlift exercises from a video or on-line virtual program, still many believe the best way to learn is with a Personal Trainer.

A professional personal trainer can not only teach you proper technique, but gets to know you as an individual. Evaluates your progress and changes and modifies routines so that they are right for you. A personal trainer can help you with your over all lifestyle to maximize your weightlifting goals. A personal trainer will be able to make recommendations on the best diet to go along with your weightlifting, the best nutritional supplements, and the other types of workouts you should be doing to enhance and compliment your weightlift routines.

So where do I find a Personal Trainer and what should I look for in one? The best place to start looking is at your neighborhood healthclub, most professional gyms have personal trainers on staff and will develop a program of sessions with one as part of a membership package. If they do not have trainers on staff they will be sure to be able to recommend one to you. Personal Trainers ought to be certified by a trustworthy health institute such as ACSM -The American College of Sports Medicine, or ACE - The American Council for Exercise. You should get information about your trainers background, how long has he or she been a trainer, how many students do they have. Ask for personal references. Find out if they hold any other degrees, awards or certifications in fitness. If you have specific goals in mind or specific medical conditions be sure you are working with a trainer who has knowledge and experince in these arenas. For example if you primary goal is Bodybuilding, you do not want to work with powerlifting coach. If you have a back injury, or heart-trouble you want to work with a trainer who knows about workouts and weightlifting routines designed for people with such conditions. Before you pick a trainer it might be a good idea to just observe some training sessions at the gym, and see which trainer seems to be using teaching techniques you like or has a personality that you would be comfortable with.

A weightlifting session with a personal trainer will usually be around 60 minutes. The first time you meet with the trainer will be used to asses your physical abilities, focus on your goals, and get prepared for any special needs you may have. You will likely be weighed and body measurements will be taken to have a "baseline". Subsequent sessions will be devoted to a customized routine of aerobic exercises and muscle training for your specific weightlifting goals.

Safety Tips for Weight Lifting

Weightlifting can be fun. Weightlifting is a great way to get in shape and stay in shape. But like any physical activity weightlifting is not without some inherent risks. The good news is that most of not all of the potentials injuries that can result form weightlifting can be avoided by practicing good technique an observing proper safety precautions.

The most common injury related to weightlifting is a back injury. Almost all weightlifting related back injuries occur due to improper technique or lifting beyond ones limitations. Both situations can be easily avoided. If yo are prone to a back injury or already have an injured back perhaps you should avoid the weight lifting exercises that are the most common causes of back injury such as Squats or Deadlifts.

For beginners it is far less likely to use improper technique that can result in an injury, by working out on a weight machine, then using free weights. If you do not have the opportunity to be properly trained in the use of free weights, the machines are the way to go. A machine forces you into the right stance or body position for any given weightlifting exercise, and there is little or no possibility of an injury due to a dropped weight while using a machine.

Whether you are weightlifting on a machine or with free weights there are several other weight lifting safety precautions you can take. If you are using free weights, always use a spotter when lifting heavy weights. If no spotter is available be sure to use equipment such as a Squat cage, or press bench that has a place to put the weights on. Weightlifters lifting either with free weights or weight machines should use weightlifting gloves. Gloves ensure a better grip on bars, and prevent blisters and other hand injuries. Wrist straps and wrist hooks can also be used to prevent hand and wrist injuries and add more support to the wrists while working out. Similarly knee braces and back belts can be used where apropos. Weight lifting shoes are a good idea to ensure proper balance and stability when lifting.

Also make sure the equipment is properly functioning. Be sure all pins and clips are secure and in the proper place. Be sure your work out area is free from obstacles and other potential hazards. Do not lift beyond your means, follow a logical progression of slowly increasing the amount of weight or reps.

Avoid the temptation to "lift to your max". Moderate soreness is OK, and should be expected from ay weightlifting session, however severe pain is not normal. If you are experiencing severe pain stop what you are doing, you are no doubt doing something wrong.

And finally, probably the best way to weightlift safely, ensure proper technique, and avoid injury is to work with a certified personal trainer.

Weight Lifting at Home Vs Gym

You are about to get started with a weightlifting program and now you are wondering should I workout in a gym or purchase home equipments and workout at home? Each have their advantages and disadvantages and experts agree it matters far less where you work out then how you workout. As long as you learn properly and lift properly you pretty much physically can get the same work out with the right weightlifting routine at home, as you can in any gym.

Home vs. Gym in a way really is part of the broader question of free weights vs. weight machines. Because a set of barbells is pretty inexpensive and does not take up much space, it really is very possible to get the same workout at home as in a gym. With proper training you can accomplish anything (and more, some would argue) with a good set of free weights as you can with weight machines. But proper training is the key, and if you are going to workout at home with free weights, you need to get yourself a good series of instructional videos, or maybe a few sessions with a personal trainer. If you are a total novice and would feel more comfortable on machines, today that does not rule out home workouts. There are good quality affordable home weightlifting machines available that do not take up nearly as much space as they used to.

The advantage of workingout at home is just that – being at home. Yo are in your own space, you can workout when you want for as long as you want. On the other hand it takes real discipline to workout regularly at home, and many people feel the need to have a gym membership to stay motivated since they don't want to feel they are wasting money. Gyms also have the advantage of trainers on staff. Some people like the social interaction of gyms, and some people really get off at showing off in a gym, while others relish the privacy of weightlifting at home. So it really comes down to a case of personal choice and personality type as to what is better for them weightlifting at home or weightlifting in a gym.

The other advantages of weightlifting in a gym however are that in a gym it is easier to cross train with other activities for cardio like aerobics or swimming. Then again many people with home gyms also own a treadmill or stationary bike, or can simply take a jog or bike ride around the block for cardio, so again personal choice. Others I have spoken with have told me that even having gone all out to set up a home gym with everything you can think of, weightlifting machine, Stairmaster, ellipticals you name it – they still found the TV and refrigerator, kids, wife, what-have-you; too distracting to really get a into a good weightlifting and strength training regimen at home. So they wound up throwing the whole shooting match on EBay and used the proceeds for a gym membership!

Best Weight Lift Routines – What the Pros Say

Weightlifting is no known to a be great workout for anybody, any sex and just about any age or fitness level. There is not a single human being on the planet above the age of 8 that can not benefit from reducing fat and building lean muscle mass. That having been said, what then is best weightlifting routine to do that? Take a look at the list I gave you at the start of this paragraph – quite a broad range of people right? And do you think a routine for a 70 year old woman whose weightlifting goal is to increase some strength and fight the effects of osteoporosis – could possibly be the same as a 24 year old competitive bodybuilder? Of course not – the best weightlifting routines are the ones that are best FOR YOU – and for your individual goals.

However with that in mind there are some general ideas that all pros agree make any weightlifting goals more achievable. It is always best to clearly define your goals and work with a professional trainer before you begin any weightlifting program. And also check with your doctor, as you should before beginning any exercise regimen.

The basic formula to successfully building lean muscle mass through weightlifting is a simple one.

- Work only one muscle group per day – and be aware of what exercises work multiple muscle groups – a tried and true formula is 5 days on 2 days off.

- Heavy Compound exercises like Squats, Deadlifts etc, work multiple muscle groups and give yo more "Bang for your Bucks, so focus on these type of exercises, unless you goal is to build specific muscles for specific sports or daily activities

- Always develop your weekly/daily routine to lift large muscle groups before small one

- Do compound weightlift exercises before isolation exercises

Again the magic of weightlifting as an exercise is that it can be used to improve overall health and physical fitness for your entire life – just ask Jack LaLanne, still pumping at 93! But a weightlifting program also can be targeted and tailor made to work specific muscle groups for specific sports, or even slow the progression of certain disease states like osteoporosis or arthritis. So without getting into specific exercises for your specific goals, experts also recommend the following for getting the most out of a general weightlifting program. Do more compound than isolation exercises, use proper form, and use heavy weights with minimal reps. The key to building muscle is to stimulate muscle growth by pushing muscles to the point of fatigue and stress – heavier weights do this more effectively. There is a misconception that if you can continue to do rep after rep with a light weight you will get "tone and definition". This is not true. Now that is not to say that doing reps of light weight has no benefit – you are getting a cardio workout doing that – but that is all you are doing – you are doing nothing to build muscle. That is where the familiar term "No Pain – No Gain" comes from. It doesn't mean that weightlifting is supposed to hurt, nor does it refer to the obvious pain you will be in the next day after your first weightlifting session. It means that in order to build muscle, muscle tissue must first be "hurt" it needs to be pushed beyond its limit – so it regrows bigger and stronger – it's really is that simple.

Weightlifting World Records

Weightlifting is a great way to be fit life. For the layperson there really is no workout routine with more overall health benefit then weightlifting. But lets not forget that weightlifting is also a competitive sport, so we thought you might be interested in some Weightlifting World Records.

As a sport, weightlifting is overseen by the IWF, International Weightlifting Federation. The records discussed in this article will be those sanctioned and validated by the IWF. The IWF was founded in 1905, however competitive weightlifting has a much longer history then that, the most ancient tests of strength were weightlifting competitions, and weightlifting, as we know it today was part of the original Greek Olympic games. Modern Olympic and professional weightlifting as sanctioned by the IWF really began to gain popularity especially in this country in the 1950's. Throughout the 1950's, '60s and into the 1970's and 80's Russian Lifters and other eastern Europeans seemed to dominate the sport. Many people are familiar with the name Vasly Alexeyev of The USSR, who in the 1970's set 80 world records and won two Olympic gold medals, and is generally recognized as the greatest powerlifter who ever lived. However patriotic Americans should also take note that a poll of IWF membership conducted in the 1980's named the USA's Tommy Kono as the greatest weightlifter in history. Kono set 26 world records, won two gold medals, one silver and remains the only competitive weightlifter to set and hold onto world records in four different weight classes

The current official record for the Men's Clean and Jerk is an impressive 579.8 lbs, held by Iranian powerlifter, Hossein Rezaradeh. The heaviest clean and jerk of all time was done by Leonid Taraneko of the then Soviet Union who in 1988 lifted 586.4 pounds. Rezardeh also holds the current record for the Snatch at 469.6 pounds. The all time heaviest recorded snatch was 476.2 pounds lifted by Antonio Kraslev of Bulgaraia in 1987. On the women's side, 402.3 pounds was clean and jerked by Gonghong Tang of China at the 2004 Olympics in Sydney.

There are many other feats of weightlifting prowess and amazing "unofficial" if you will, records in weightlifting that are quite interesting and fascinating. They certainly can keep you motivated, and who knows maybe you might want to go after one of these. According to Guinness, the record for the most bench presses in one hour is held by Eamonn Keane of Ireland who bench pressed a weight or 200lbs 1,280 times, and did 493 reps with a 100lb weight all in under 1 hour for a total of 305,300 pounds!

And Phil Pfister was named the 2006 Worlds Strongest Man in that annual competition, when in the final round he deadlifted two cars weighing a total of 728 pounds 12 times, then he defeated his opponents and gained the title by being the only man it the competition to successfully overhead lift 4 irregularly shaped stones weighing 227, 242, 275, and 294 pounds respectively.

Is there a Difference Between Weight Lifting and Body Building?

Yes. Just ask that question to a "bodybuilder" or a "weightlifter" and you will get an earful of an answer. While it is true that bodybuilders and weightlifters will both train with weights – they are two very distinct sports, with two very distinct goals in mind, especially when we are talking about them on the professional level.

A professional or competitive bodybuilder is mainly concerned with look. They are going for an overall body image that shows off lean and defined muscle mass to its greatest visual apperance. A weightlifter on the other hand is primarily concerned with lifting weights to build muscle and increase strength. Now both sports involve weight training and strength training and that is where these is crossover, and probably the reason for much of the confusion. But the way an individual trains, and by training we mean overall lifestyle, and especially as this relates to diet and nutrition, will be the greatest departure point between "weightlifters" and "bodybuilders."

The ultimate goal in a bodybuilding competition is definition, and definition as defined in the bodybuilding world means the most muscle and least amount of fat. Bodybuilders strive for 0% body fat, and while that may not be possible, many competitive bodybuilders have percentages of body fat in the 2 – 4% range. This is of a far less of a concern to a weightlifter. A weightlifter especially a competitive weightlifter wins his competition by lifting the most weight - period. So he will workout specific muscle groups to maximize the strength in the areas of their competition. In other words the muscles most important during a snatch or Deadlift. For the competitive bodybuilder on the other hand winning a competition has nothing to do with how much you can lift or how strong your muscles are, but how well your overall physique looks, and looks right together. All the muscles on a competitive bodybuilder must look symmetrical, and in proper proportion, so they must work out all parts of the body equally.

Now if you are not planning on competing in either sport the distinction may not really be that important to you. However, the discussion spells out how important it is to clearly identify your goals as to why you are lifting weights. Are you looking to improve physique? Enhance strength and stamina? Or maybe a little or both? If you are not a competitor, it really matters less what your call yourself, then what you want to accomplish with weightlifting. When you know what you want to get out of a weightlifting program you can then design a series of routines, exercises and lifestyle changes, to meet those goals accordingly.

Aerobics and Weight Lifting

Traditional fitness and exercise gurus have often slammed weightlifting as having a minimal impact on cardiovascular health and overall health, because of its lack of being an aerobic exercise. Current medical thinking has not only debunked this myth, with several studies that prove there is an aerobic content to general weightlifting, there is now also a whole school of thought among the workout community that could be considered aerobic weightlifting. Aerobic weightlifting combines the best of traditional weightlifting exercises and techniques, with traditional cardio workouts, for improved overall health and fitness.

Traditional weight lifting or weight training insist on a rest period between each set of exercises. Aerobic weight lifting borrows from the philosophy of circuit training. In simple terms it means keep moving don't stop, move form one exercise to the next without a rest period. This increases the need for blood infused oxygen to power you muscles, and forces the lungs and heart to work harder, effectively an aerobic work out. If you are workingout at home and do not have a multi-station gym machine and cannot move directly form one weightlifting exercise to the next without stopping to change weight plates on your barbells, you can get the cardio benefit by doing a little traditional aerobic exercises between sets, like skipping rope.

You will find that you will be less sore after doing this kind of aerobic weightlifting. This type of weightlifting promotes the removal of toxins and poisons in the body. During a traditional weightlifting workout when the muscles are at rest during the rest cycle, these toxins are given the ability to build up in the muscles, by keeping the blood moving with aerobics, they are more likely to be flushed out. Yet the continuous lifting does keep the muscles fatigued which is the basis for them to rebuild as in traditional weightlifting.

Combining aerobics with weightlifting in one form or another has proven health benefits, especially for middle-aged people. A recent study published in the American Journal of Preventive Medicine found that people in the study aged 55-75 lowered the degree of metabolic syndrome – a condition combining diabetes and heart disease – 41 percent, with a 6 month program of aerobic exercises and weightlifting.

Aerobic weightlifting can break the monotony of a traditional weight lifting routine. Aerobic weightlifting through circuit training can help introduce people to weightlifting who otherwise felt it was not for them. By working out with aerobic styled weightlifting you really do achieve the best of both worlds, you can get all of the cardiovascular and fat burning benefits of traditional aerobics, and the building up of lean muscle mass, increased strength and stamina of traditional weightlifting, all in one workout

Weight Lifting and Raising Metabolism

Why is weightlifting such a great way to stay fit? It isn't just because of the great look you will get – weightlifting has a multitude of health benefits because weightlifting raises your metabolism.

Metabolism, we know it is the problem word when it comes to trying to lose weight. The slower our metabolism the harder it is to lose fat and keep it off. Now there are hundreds of theories as to why one person has a slower metabolism then another. Certainly lifestyle and eating habits have a lot to do with it. As do genetic factors. Plus everyone's metabolism, no matter how good shape they are in, slows with age. There is however one undeniable biological fact – muscle raises your metabolism, fat does not. Muscle is what is known as active tissue; even at rest muscle consumes energy. In the body consumption of energy means burning of calories. The more muscle you have the more calories you burn. And weightlifting builds muscle.

Now once you have become a metabolic fat burning machine, with increased lean muscle from weightlifting, you receive all the other perks of that higher metabolism. Other exercises will become easier, and you will continue to burn fat. Now this is important because if you really want to raise that metabolism keep it up there and stay healthy, it takes more then just the boost you will get form weightlifting. Experts agree that to raise you metabolic rate and keep it higher, it is best to combine weightlifting with other exercises and increased physical activity, and the added strength one gets form weightlifting make this that much easier. Want a sure way to lower your metabolism, how about an injury that takes you off your feet and puts you on the couch for a few weeks? Weightlifting correctly can help to prevent other sports related injuries by strengthening joints, bones and muscles.

And finally, while weightlifting and exercise are the surest way to give your metabolism a boost, you also must adjust your diet and limit your fat intake. The biggest mistake most people make whether they are active weightlifters/exercisers or not – is to skip breakfast. Your metabolism has dropped during rest overnight; it will stay low and go into "starvation" mode if not given adequate nutrition in the morning. The best way to keep a revved up metabolism going is to give your body constant fuel to burn, and eat small amounts of food all day long. Think about it like keeping a fire roaring in the fire place, keep throwing in wood and it will continue to consume fuel and burn bright and powerful – don't feed it and what happens? It will slowly die down until it goes…Out.

Weightlifting for Women over 40

For a long time women, even women who loved to exercise and stay in shape, feared weightlifting, and preferred to just do "cardio and aerobics" for fear of gaining "big muscles and looking like a man". Today most women realize this is a myth, and know the benefits of weightlifting and building lean muscle. But they may not realize that these benefits extend into the forties and beyond. In fact recent studies have shown that the benefits of weightlifting can do a lot to reduce the effect of aging. And what woman doesn't want to do that?

According to a recent report in the Journal of the American Medical Association (JAMA) it has been found that weightlifting and strength training for women can help them perform better with the tasks of everyday living as they age. It is a biological fact that woman have smaller muscles, frailer bones, and more body fat than men. As we age we tend to lose muscle mass, lose bone density, and of course gain fat due to slower metabolism. Since women have less to start with, they are at greater risk of certain age related condition due to bone and muscle loss, such as osteoporosis, loss of balance, and frail skeletons. Older woman are at far greater risk of bone fractures then their male counterparts. Muscle and bone strengthening exercises, such as weightlifting has been shown to significantly reduce these risks, especially in postmenopausal woman.

Weightlifting has been shown to do more for woman trying to lose weight and keep it off then aerobics alone. While aerobic exercise will burn more fat initially upon working out then weightlifting. Studies by specialists in Sports Medicine have proven that the body continues to burn calories up to two hours after a workout with weights, while the effects of a traditional aerobic workout only last about half hour.

Woman begin to lose muscle mass in their 30's, it accelerates in the 40's and gets even more rapid with the hormonal changes that occur with menopause. As muscle is lost fat takes its place. Metabolism slows, and even without eating more or exercising less, women in their 40's will start to gain weight. This process can be reversed with weightlifting and gaining back lean muscle and you know what ladies, that doesn't mean you will look "manly" but id does mean you will look and feel younger!

Weight training at any age has been shown to be good for your heart, but this too is especially good news for woman in their 40's. As a general rule most woman are not at risk for heart disease prior to the age of 40. But over 40 that risk begins to increase. According to the American Heart Association weightlifting has been shown to significantly decrease several of the risk factors for heart attack; including lowering blood pressure, and reduction of fat, lipids and cholesterol build up in the blood

Weight Lifting on the Beach

Ahh... sun, sand and surf. While there has been much debate over what is the best place to weightlift either at home or in the gym – for many weightlifters, those aren't even in the running. For them their favorite place to weightlift is on the beach.

And when it comes to weightlifting and working out on the beach there is probably no place more famous or more well known then California's Muscle Beach. Jack LaLanne and Vic Tanney are only two of the fitness legends that made the place famous. In its heyday muscle-bound stars from Buster Crabbe (Flash Gordon) and Johnny Weissmuller (Tarzan) to Steve Reeves (Hercules) all showed their stuff on Muscle Beach. And of course current Governor of California Arnold Scharzenegger was once a common site at Venice Beaches Outdoor Body Building Competitions.

Muscle Beach is still an extremely popular work out spot for fitness enthusiasts of all shapes and sizes. Located in Santa Monica the beach has been fully restored and features many state of the art work out stations. It even has scaled down stations and "Jungle Gyms" on a padded ground for kids. The site is still a popular one for many on going bodybuilding competitions. Joe Wheatly Productions holds weekly competitions at Muscle Beach every Sunday afternoon from August through October. As always in the tradition of the original Muscle Beach the public is free to attend. If you want to get a look at some of the great bods on the guys (and gals) who frequent Muscle Beach check out http://www.pbase.com/markwp/santamonica.

The bonds between weightlifting, body building, Muscle Beach and Hollywood were more formally tied in 2001 when several actors who portrayed the legendary strongman Hercules were given special recognition at the 2001 Muscle Beach Competition. Actors who portrayed the Sandal Wearing Greek Demigod, Mark Forest, Ed Fury Mickey Hargitay, Reg Lewis and Peter Lupus -who was probably better known for playing Circus Strongman Willy Armitage for several seasons on the "Mission Impossible" TV series - were all present to accept the Special Achievement Award.

California isn't the only Coast with a popular Weightlifting and Bodybuilding Destination. In November Gold's Gym Holds their annual "Muscle Camp" Competition on Miami Florida's South Beach. Normally the playground of celebrities, sports stars, and other "Rich and Famous" types, for one weekend in November the beach becomes home to some of the top names in the body building world including; Jay Cutler, Shawn Ray and Milos Sarcev. It is a three-day event with training sessions, tips from the pros and day and evening competitions on the beach.

Weightlifting for Men Over 50

Recent studies have proven that you are never too old to start weight training and benefit from the wealth of physical benefits of weightlifting. In fact if you have never done any weightlifting or strength training and are over 50, now is the best time to start.

Men lose muscle mass as they age - it's a fact. For each decade of adult life if we do not exercise we lose 5 to 7 pounds of muscle, most guys as they age put on at least that much or more in fat as metabolism slows. Weightlifting and strength training has been shown to not only slow this process, but can replace much of lost muscle tissue. As you build muscle tissue, metabolism increases, and many benefits result. Many of the conditions that come with aging: osteoporosis, arthritis, high blood pressure, heart diseases can actually be prevented and in many cases even reversed, with an appropriate weightlifting regimen.

Total joint replacement surgery such as the knee and hip, is probably the most common surgery in men over 50. A proper regimen of strength training and weight lifting has been proven in study after study to reduce the need for such surgery, as increased muscle strength also helps preserve and in many cases stop the deterioration of weight bearing joints. Also one of the most common injuries among older people is sprained or broken wrists and ankles due to falls. Weightlifting has been shown to prevent these injuries in more then one way. Weightlifting strengthens bones, making them less fragile, and less susceptible to fracture in the event of fall. And also weightlifting improves balance and leg strength, making a fall far less likely in the first place. Members of the medical and the fitness community now generally agree that probably the best preventative and anti-aging medicine there is is weightlifting and strength training. Of course especially for older men who may be workingout with weights for the first time it is highly recommended that you consult with your physician before starting any kind of exercise routine.

Then once you are good to go you can join a gym or you can get a good set of barbells and begin resistance training and weightlifting in your own home. If you have never lifted before and since being over 50 you may be at greater risk of certain injuries – joining a gym and working with a personal trainer to learn proper technique and weightlifting safety is probably a good idea. A personal trainer can also help to tailor a weight lifting routine to your specific goals and personal needs. Also while many professional weightlifters disdain weight machines, for older beginners they are great because they are easier to use, insure proper form and technique, and can be used by just about anyone with little or no instruction or prior weightlifting experince.

Protect Your Hands While Weight Lifting

Next to back injury probably one of the most common injuries in weight lifting is injury to the hands. Even when lifting with perfect technique the hands take a lot of abuse when weightlifting and it is very ironic that where weightlifting has been shown to actually prevent or in some cases reverse arthritis in some joints like the elbows, knees and shoulders, it can cause arthritis in the hands. With over 50 bones in the hand, hand pain is certainly quite common among weightlifters.

But most hand pain that is the result of weightlifting can be avoided with the use of proper protective equipment like weightlifting gloves. Weightlifting gloves are designed to prevent hand injuries and ensure a better grip on weightlifting gloves. Basic weightlifting gloves offer simple protection from blisters and calluses and give a surer grip on the bar. They are inexpensive, usually less then ten dollars, and probably made of leather with a stretch material like spandex for a sure fit around the wrist. They do not differ that much form other sport or driving gloves. Moving up in quality (and price) are what are usually called "performance" gloves, that are like the basic or standard weightlifting gloves with the added feature of some type of additional support for the wrist. They may also have some padding in the palm for additional comfort. Then there are weightlifting gloves that have built in hooks or straps as an additional safety feature. Lifting straps prevent hand and wrist pain and also allow more reps and longer workouts. For serious lifters there are professional weightlifting gloves. These are made for anyone who trains with heavy weights more than 5 days a week. They have adjustable wrist supports, padding, rubber cushions and reinforced no-slip areas in the palms. They will provide the maximum protection support and comfort for the more than casual lifter and sell in the 30.00 to 40.00 range.

If you already have arthritis in the hands and wrists, there is a new series of gloves on the market specifically designed to improve the grip strength of people with hand arthritis and allow them to keep lifting. Made of neoprene rubber with thicker hand pads then in most performance gloves and specialized wrist supports, these gloves act like shock absorbers for the hands while weightlifting. These gloves are recommended by fitness trainers over standard weightlifting gloves for any lifter, not just those with arthritis. The padding and support of these gloves allow a lifter to do more reps and work out longer because of increased grip strength and less hand pain.

Best Weight Lifting Routines for Skiers

One of the things that makes weightlifting such a great exercise is that it not only is the best workout you can get for overall health and fitness, but since there are isolation weightlifting and strength training exercises, you can tailor make routines to improve your performance in any sport. For example skiing.

People who do not ski regularly may not realize how physically demanding a sport it is. And we are not talking about extreme downhill here, even basic recreational skiing taxes muscle groups in both the upper and lower body, and requires good balance.

If you do not workout with weights regularly, as we recommend for all people, it is extremely important that you work your muscles for skiing. Why? Because for most people skiing is a once a year activity, and if you have been sitting around on your duff all year before that first ski trip, you certainly are not in any condition to face a downhill. Weight training and weight lifting routines that can add to your flexibility and muscle strength are recommended for skiers. You also want to strength train especially for the quads. Strong quads can help protect yo from the most common skiing injuries like damage to the knees joints from sudden stops or turns.

Leg lifts ad leg presses are probably the best exercise for strengthening quads. You can do leg lifts or leg extension on the leg station on a weight machine, or with a barbell and weigh bench outfitted for leg extensions. Sit with back firm against the back of the pad; slip your ankles tight under the footpad. With you back straight and firm do at least 3 sets of 10 reps at a comfortable weight. As your strength increases, build it up to 12 – 15 reps. Also try to 4-8 reps with each leg individually at half weight. Leg Presses are also very effective for building up muscle in the quads. There are several positions for leg presses on most multi-gym stations; any and all of them are valuable weightlifting exercises for skiers. The same machine or bench that you used for leg extensions, can also be used for hamstring strengthening, another exercise of value to skiers. Flip over onto your belly; slip your legs under the footpads to do hamstring curls. Skiers are also going to benefit from strengthening the calf muscles. Most gyms will have a calf machine, but you can also accomplish the same work out with a barbell across the shoulders. And if you really want to get a compete lower body workout – squats and lunges are the ticket – but these can be difficult exercises and not recommended for beginners who have had no prior weightlifting experince or training.

Try to do these exercises at least two days a week, with two days off to rest and rebuild. You might want to take a day in between to work the upper body. It is not a good idea to work the same muscle groups two days in a row. But with a little simple weight training you'll be ready for the slopes in no time.

Best Weight Lifting Routines for Tennis Players

Tennis itself is a great and fun way to exercise and stay in shape for people of all ages. But what exercises can you do to improve you tennis game? Simple answer - weightlifting and strength training. One of the main reasons that fitness and health professionals alike have begun to recognize weightlifting and strength training as the perfect exercise, is that it is not only is the best workout you can get for overall wellness, but with isolation weightlifting and strength training exercises, and even compound exercises that target specific muscle groups, you can customize weightlifting routines to improve your performance for any game – even tennis.

At first glance you might think that strength training and therefore weightlifting exercises for tennis players would concentrate on arms and grip strength for better power and control of your shots. And while that is true and all tennis players will work the arms and upper body – pros and enthusiasts all agree that a sharp tennis game relies as much an speed and agility as it does on the power of your forehand or serve.

While there was a time when it was believed that athletes other then bodybuilders or weightlifters should not weightlift because they will get too "muscle bound" or too heavy to perform, that is generally a "fitness myth" that has since been debunked. Quickness of the legs, balance, agility, the ability to stop quick and turn, and shift directions – all important to the tennis player – are all a function of muscle strength. The stronger your leg muscle the more force it exerts against the court, the faster you go to get to that ball – simple physics. Strong leg muscles, quads and calf, and hamstrings, also mean that it is less likely you will experince the most common tennis playing injuries like, torn ligaments.

A weightlifting routine that you would follow for basic strength training and overall good health is great for tennis. Doing a circuit of full body workouts both to improve upper and lower body, will all benefit your tennis game. While having stronger specific muscles will improve specific aspects of your game as described, an overall increase in lean muscle mass as the result of a regular strength training and weightlifting routine will improve your strength and stamina, will improve you cardio function, and make you lungs work more efficiently. All factors that are extremely important in a rigorous activity like a few sets of tennis. If you are a regular tennis player – you will "love" the "advantage" that weightlifting will give you.

Best Weightlifting Routines for Track

Years ago the conventional wisdom was that athletes, especially athletes that relied on speed like track and filed stars – should not weightlift or strength train. There was the thinking that they become too "muscle bound" and cannot perform well due to heavy or bulky muscle. Well Sports Medicines practioners and professional trainers know that that is simply not true. Weightlifting and strength training can and does improve the ability of anybody, any athlete in any sport – even track and field.

Today track runners will all strength train. They recognize that strong legs and lithe body made of lean muscle – is what a track runner needs. And you can get that kind of endomorphic physique through weightlifting.

Speed is probably the most essential element to the track competitor. And speed workouts are what are called for when it comes to the best kind of weightlifting routines for the runner.

In weightlifting, speed workouts refer to interval training. It is a training style of weightlifting designed to increase speed, stamina, and endurance making it the ideal training method for track and field athletes. In interval training the weightlifter will push themselves hard and fast to their limits. Interval training is the best way to burn fat and raise metabolism, which is why it is the preferred method for runners. In interval weightlifting, the weightlifter uses time as a marker, you work a certain exercise to the max for that period of time, and then follow it with an easier workout for another period of time. Determining the maximum and what exercises should be performed at what intervals is the key to successful interval weight training. And therefore interval training is not something that should be attempted on your own, but rather you should work with a professional trainer or fitness coach to develop a program that is right for your particular needs.

But lets say you are not a competitive runner, just someone who runs as hobby, for other fitness, or does the occasional marathon. Weightlifting and strength training is for you too. While interval training is a preferred method for the pros, the average runners need not weightlift at that intensity. However, any runner can benefit from the improved strength and stamina that will come from weightlifting. The single most effective weightlifting exercise for improving just about any sport related to track and field – Squats. Ironman triathletes, and other track and field and fitness pros have called Squats "The Perfect Exercise" because when done correctly they work every major muscle group critical to sports like running, swimming, and bike riding.

Best Weightlifting Routines for Baseball

When it comes to team sports you probably envision that only football training camps have a huge weight room. And yes a lot of NFL players will strength train and bodybuild much the same way as bodybuilders and weightlifters, but there isn't a sport out there whose players can't benefit form weightlifting and strength training – and baseball is no exception. Have you looked at the arms on any power hitter lately?

Now controversies about performance enhancing drugs not withstanding there is not a ball player out there, professional or otherwise that doesn't realize they need to get an edge over their competition, and weightlifting is the surest, safest, and legalist way to do that. Strength training and weightlifting improve overall strength, improve stamina, improve speed, coordination and balance, and help to prevent injuries. What baseball player doesn't want that? Al baseball players will strength train and weightlift today as part of their workout routines.

Since baseball is the kind of sport that uses various muscle groups, and that is what fitness pros refer to as an "on again off again sport" where you can be standing still for example and then suddenly need super quick burst of speed to sprint to a ball, or steal base – trainers agrees that for baseball yo need to vary your workouts as mush as possible. Use free weight and machines, and even other strength training pieces of equipment like medicine balls, clubs, and resistance trainers. Medicine balls are an ideal strength-training device for baseball players. A work out with a 9 to 10 pound medicine ball builds stamina and power. It teaches your muscles how to work together in unison. Atypical medicine ball exercise goes something like this. Grab the medicine ball about chest height as if you were going to pass it to someone like a basketball – squat down and press the ball against a wall, and jump as many times as you can with the ball against the wall for thirty seconds. Baseball players should train with heavier weights on their lower bodies, and lighter weights on the upper muscle groups. Baseball players should be particularly conscious of exercises that involve the pushing and pulling of the shoulder muscles, and do these with care to avoid shoulder injuries.

As a player or fan of baseball you have no doubt heard of the rotator cuff, it is one of the most common injuries that sidelines a ball player. Specific weightlifting exercises can be done to strengthen the rotator cuff, and help to prevent these injuries. The key to weightlifting and strength training for the baseball player is to build functional strength. As a ball player you will be required to star, stop and explode with bursts of power, lean muscle mass gives you the strength and the energy to do that. Weightlifting builds lean muscle mass.

Best Weightlifting Routines for Soccer

They don't call them "soccer moms" for nothing. Soccer has become one of the most popular team spots and athletic activities among kids and teens today. And if you really want to see them improve their game, and prevent injuries, you should have your teen age soccer players get into a good weightlifting and strength training routine.

Soccer is a sport that uses many muscle groups. It is physically demanding, requiring great stamina and aerobic abilities combined with explosive burst of strength and power for running and kicking. Weight lifting improves all of these areas. Of course soccer require lower body and leg strength for kicking, jumping and running. Upper body strength is needed for shielding the ball and defending against opponents. Now maximum strength is good for a soccer player, being strong is certainly never going to hurt your game. But maximum strength is not what its all about – just being strong enough to say lift a heavy weight as in weightlifting, doesn't say anything about your speed –and in soccer speed is as important as strength. So yo must weight train with workouts that are designed to increase your speed as much as your strength.

The best way to train for speed and strength for soccer or really any sport for that mater is to apply a concept that is called plyometrics. Plyometrics basically uses the theory that a muscle that is sufficiently stretched before it is worked out will contract that much faster, faster contractions faster movement – in essence more speed!   But plyometrics work by taking existing strength and converting it into speed and power though more efficient contraction of muscles, so the initial strength must be there first. Therefore, still most soccer coaches sophisticated enough to understand plyometrics and apply the techniques to their players still recommend an effective program of all around strengthening though weightlifting first.

Of course the areas of the body you will want to most strengthen as a soccer player are the legs, hips, thighs, calves, back and glutes. For weightlifters that spells Squats –squats are probably the single most effective weightlifting exercise for building up lower body strength, power and endurance. Leg lifts; leg presses and hamstring curls should also be part of the regular weightlifting routine for any soccer player. Circuit training is recommended for soccer players this allows them to work many muscle groups in an appropriate order, and even simulates the switching of one muscle group to another, which is often the case during a soccer match.

Printed by Libri Plureos GmbH in Hamburg, Germany